THE
ETRUSCANS

THE

ETRUSCANS

AGNES CARR VAUGHAN

BARNES
&NOBLE
BOOKS
NEW YORK

Originally published as *Those Mysterious Etruscans*.

Copyright © 1964 by Agnes Carr Vaughan
All rights reserved.

This edition published by Barnes & Noble, Inc.,
by arrangement with Doubleday & Company, Inc.
a division of Bantam Doubleday Dell.

1993 Barnes & Noble Books

ISBN 1-56619-276-5

Printed and bound in the United States of America

M 9 8 7 6 5 4 3 2

FOR

ISABELLE S. TAYLOR

my psychic editor

who prefers the Etruscan

uknus to *sunku*

The noise of worldly fame is but a blast of wind
That blows from diverse points, and shifts its name
Shifting the point it blows from.

DANTE, *tr.* Cary

Contents

Part Three: The Bronze Age

Part Four: The Iron Age

Introduction

Even in antiquity, the Etruscans were surrounded by an aura of mystery. No one really knew who they were or where they came from; only that they were a people who, some two thousand years ago, lived and flourished greatly, though briefly, in the land we now know as Italy, but which in earlier days was called Vitelia (calf-land). The Greek and Roman historians had many theories about the origin of these strange people, who spoke an unknown tongue, and these theories they have handed down to us to mull over, as many scholars already have done.

A recent theory holds that the Etruscans developed from two ethnic strains—a Western strain from the Danube basin, and an Eastern strain from Anatolia—and that they came in two successive waves to Italy. The blending of these ethnic strains, in as far as they did blend in the new land, produced the people we call Etruscans; it also produced many synonymous words, such as *vinum* and *ena,* both meaning wine.

The rise and fall of the Etruscans was incredibly swift; almost as if that fate in which they believed had marked the path they were to walk and, when they had reached its end, had destined them to disappear, as their mythical law-giver Tages disappeared when he had fulfilled his mission.

Various reasons have been advanced to account for this swift transit of the Etruscan people from the unknown to nothingness. Among these reasons four seem to be justifiable; their inability to weld themselves into a nation, their slavish obedience to the Tagetic Doctrine, as interpreted by their *haruspices,* or soothsayers, their clinging to obsolete weapons, and the blows they suffered under the type of colonization the Romans evolved.

The ancient Greek poet Hesiod, who lived in the harsh land of Boeotia, introduced into his epic poem, *Works and Days,* the commonly held theory that the world was undergoing a steady deterioration from an early Golden Age of purity and innocence to an inferior age of bronze. To the gold, silver, and bronze stages of the world he adds his own age, when "black iron" had become known. These symbols seem poignantly adaptable to the life and death of the Etruscan people as an ethnic entity.

The Golden Age of the Etruscans was one of growth and hope; they had reached, as it were, their Promised Land. The future held no terrors, for they believed what their soothsayers told them: that they would become gods. Their Silver Age was one of lessened hope, or as Hesiod expressed the theory that had come down to his day, "less noble by far." Writers often speak of the Etruscans as Men of Bronze, but when Hesiod spoke of the Age of Bronze, he was thinking in spiritual terms applicable to all peoples in a certain stage of national life, when they have become "brazen."

Last and saddest of all comes the Iron Age, when men take the law into their own hands. For the Etruscans, the Age of Iron was the age of Roman conquest and colonization, conquest of a people who had lifted Rome from her swamps and taught her almost, if not all, that enabled her, ultimately, to become the Imperial Mistress of the world, and to remain on that high pinnacle until her time came to fall.

The material of this book, which is intended for the general reader, has been drawn from classical sources, from modern authorities, from the Etruscan tombs that may still be visited, and from the museums. Naturally, it has not been possible to include all the available material. I have selected what I trust will present an horizontal, rather than the usual vertical, picture of those mysterious people of a bygone age who have aroused so much interest in our world of today. Since it has not suited my purpose to enter into a discussion of the remarkable technological achievement of the Lerici Foundation, which has speeded up archaeological excavations in Italy, I have omitted all mention of the Foundation.

I owe the reader a word of explanation about the genealogy of the semi-legendary Tarquins who are connected with the early history of Etruscan Rome. Some historians regard the Tarquins as grandfather and grandson; others as father and son. Chiefly because of the dates the historians give us, I have represented Tarquin the First and Tarquin the Proud as grandfather and grandson.

Gathering the material for this book has been an enjoyable experience, largely because my search led me across Europe, from the National Museum in Naples to the British Museum in London. For warm assistance and encouragement along the way, I wish to take this opportunity to thank Director Richard A. Kimball of the American Academy in Rome, Mrs. Kimball, and members of the staff. I am particularly grateful to La Signora Longobardi, whom I learned to value as both librarian and friend, to La Principessa Rospigliosi, to Mr. Ernest Nash in Rome, without whose help I should not have seen a photostat of the Book of the Mummy, and to Dr. Carla B. Tocci of Columbia University for reminding me of Pliny's claim that he had three souls because he could speak three languages: Greek, Latin, and some Etruscan.

I also wish to express my appreciation to Dr. Marie-Thérèse d'Alverney of the Bibliothèque Nationale in Paris, Dr. Raymond Schoder, S.J., of Loyola University, and Mr. Lawrence H. Cherney of Long Island City. I wish also to thank the directors of the Gregorian Museum of the Vatican, the National Museum of the Villa Giulia in Rome, the Archaeological Museums in Florence, Tarquinia, and Chiusi, the Louvre in Paris, the British Museum in London, and the Art Reference Bureau in Ancram, New York. I am also grateful to Miss Iris C. Love and to Miss Frederica Wachsberger of New York

City for access to their Villanovan and Etruscan collection.

My thanks would not be complete without mentioning Dr. Clara W. Crane for her critical reading of my manuscript, Miss Elizabeth Otis for many reasons, La Contessa Lea Anna Lelli who did much to make my stay in Rome pleasant and profitable, and finally my invaluable typists, Barbara E. Doten and Kathryn M. Baker.

My particular indebtedness is acknowledged in the dedication.

PART ONE

THE GOLDEN AGE

". . . a golden race of mortal men. . . . When they died,
it was as though they were overcome with sleep. . . ."

HESIOD, *Works and Days*

I

Etruria and Her Secret Mounds

Centuries ago, long before the birth of Christ, a mysterious people, famed in legend and in history, inhabited that part of Italy known today as Tuscany. But both legend and history spoke of the Tuscany of today, that rich center of Italy lying between two of her rivers, the Tiber and the Arno, as Etruria; and they called the people who lived there by names as varied as the accounts men still give in their books, seeking, all of them, to discover who these mysterious people really were and why they disappeared before the might of Rome.

They called themselves Rasenna, a name long since vanished, except as that of a chain of mountains near Arezzo in Tuscany. The Greeks called them Tyrrheni or Tyrseni (both names are used) and held them in bad repute; we envy them, perhaps, the life they lived in those far-off days when they expected, in some mysterious way, to become gods. For this was what their sooth-sayers had taught them, long before they left their distant home, to dwell for a time in Lydia, where the Pactolus River ran with gold.

But it was in central Etruria, that small fertile area between the Tiber and the Arno, that Etruscan social, political, and religious life grew strong, and from central Etruria that it spread vigorously. For Etruscan culture continued to flourish even after the people had lost their political independence and become absorbed in Rome, even after the rest of Italy had forgotten them. Though as an ethnic entity the Etruscans have been lost for over two thousand years, they have left behind them traces of their passing which no one can ignore: the huge, grass-grown mounds of earth, the *tumuli* of the archaeologists, that form so distinctive a feature of the Tuscan landscape. Under these great mounds, most of them dating between the seventh and the fifth centuries, many a noble Etruscan has slept undisturbed through the ages, but whether he has ever become a god or not, no one, not even the cleverest archaeologist, has ever discovered.

If the people we call Etruscans came to Italy from overseas, as immigrants, or refugees, or pirates, in few ships or in many, they would have found the western coast of the new country an excellent place for establishing a beachhead. The coast is as jagged as that of Crete. Promontories, alternating with flat, sandy beaches, run far out to sea all the way from the peninsula of Sorrento in the south to the hill city of Populonia in the north.

Again, if they came from overseas, these invaders would not have been quick to venture inland; promontories were safer for new-comers to the land. When they did move inland, seeking wood for houses, beasts for food and perhaps for clothing, they found a land rich in natural resources: forests that seemed inexhaustible, minerals, copper and iron especially, hot and cold springs, and valleys well-watered for growing grain. The landscape could not have appeared as inviting to them as it does today to the new arrival in Italy; it would have lacked the purple of the grape and the silvery-green of the olive trees, since both the grape and the olive are believed to have come with the Etruscans into Italy. But they would have seen peaks of yellowish or pinkish tufa, the solidified volcanic ash; and they would have seen russet beeches, tall green pine trees, and perhaps expanses of golden wheat and red poppies.

Ever since the fifth century B.C. the problem of Etruscan origins has troubled both ancient and modern scholars.

Herodotus, a Greek historian of the fifth century B.C., seems to

4

have been the first to inquire seriously into the origin of the Etruscan people. He felt sure that the Tyrrheni, as he called them, came originally from Lydia in Asia Minor—Anatolia, as it is known today.

The story Herodotus tells is that during a prolonged famine in Lydia the people invented games, among them the game of dice, to distract them from their hunger. These games they played throughout two whole days, eating nothing on either day; then on each third day they ate their apportioned food. For eighteen years the Lydians managed to exist in this way. Finally the king, grown desperate, divided his people into two groups: one group to stay at home, the other to leave the country and seek new lands to till for food. Lots were drawn to decide which group should go and which should stay. The king put himself at the head of those who were to stay and appointed his son, Tyrrhenus, to find new homes for those who were to go.

Tyrrhenus, Herodotus says, led his people down to Smyrna on the coast. There the Lydians built ships and set sail. Eventually they reached the western coast of Italy. Today the Tyrrhenian Sea perpetuates the name of the young prince.

Between the safe promontories and the great islands of Sardinia and Corsica in the Tyrrhenian Sea lie smaller islands that furnished stepping-stones to the rich deposits of minerals desired by the newcomers. Voracious pirates, men called them in those early days, when even the distant coast of Sicily suffered their depredations. Today we call them Etruscans, for Etruscan domination of the inland seas is no longer a legend, but a fact of archaeology, confirmed by the number of foreign objects discovered within the great mounds.

Until the time of the Emperor Augustus the account by Herodotus of the origin of the Etruscans was generally accepted. Then Dionysius of Halicarnassus cast doubt upon his fellow-countryman's story by insisting that the Etruscans were an ancient Italic people who had always lived in Central Italy and who called themselves Rasenna.

5

Their language was not Lydian, he noted; their laws were not Lydian; their gods were not Lydian. They must, he felt certain, have been a people indigenous to Italy. From Augustinian times until today many have accepted the account of Dionysius rather than that of Herodotus.

The Roman historian Tacitus believed, with Herodotus, that Etruria became the new home of the emigrating Lydians; deputies from Sardis, he recalls, once recited before the Roman Senate an Etruscan decree to prove their blood kinship "on the ground of the early colonization of Etruria by the Lydians."

Until recently modern speculation has ranged among the three possibilities: the fifth-century view of Herodotus that the Etruscans came from overseas; the view of Dionysius of Halicarnassus that they were an indigenous people; and the view held by no less a person than the great German scholar, Niebuhr, that they came down from the North over the Eastern Alps.

In 1961, a provocative new book appeared, *Les Étrusques Commencent à Parler,* the result of thirty years of study by its author, Dr. Zacharie Mayani of the University of Paris. The first British edition, translated by Patrick Evans, was published simultaneously in 1962 in London and Toronto. Though fascinating in its linguistic breadth and in its many new interpretations (particularly of the symbols, one to six, on Etruscan dice) one feels at times that some interpretations are a trifle far-fetched.

Mayani's method has been, primarily, to compare the phonetic, morphological, and semantic similarities of the Albanian and the Etruscan languages. His complete study is, however, as he states in his preface, "concerned with Albanians, Illyrians, Etruscans, and their respective languages." His study has led Mayani to conclude that the Etruscan language is essentially Indo-European, and that the Etruscan inscriptions show two currents flowing together to form "that strange civilization: one from the Danube and one from Anatolia." The Etruscans, the "men of bronze," he feels, never succeeded in erasing the marks of their origin; it shows in their weapons, their use of the pillar in their tombs, their love of poly-

6

chromy in decorative art; and it shows even more markedly in their portrayal of animals, and above all in their originality.

These two currents, one from the Danube basin, the other from Anatolia (as Herodotus believed) eventually formed a heterogenous people in the new land which we call Etruria and in which they tried to make a home. Their heterogeneity, Dr. Mayani also feels, was one reason, probably the most important one, why the Etruscans failed to become a nation.

Perhaps a theory of Toynbee's may be of some interest at this point; he cites the Etruscans as a possible example of the effect of migration overseas on a transplanted group. Since usually only the most courageous survive, their descendants are likely to remain a vigorous people, while those who stay behind often deteriorate and become lost to history.

One might add that such descendants are apt to cling to the old ways and to the old beliefs, at least until they feel themselves securely established in the new land. Many parallels between the Etruscans and the early peoples of the Near East seem to indicate that this is what happened in ancient Etruria.

Archaeology has shown that Etruria was once densely populated. Her first cities were built on promontories, and in narrow ravines and plateaus that were protected on one side by a river, which provided transportation to the coast, where their port installations were located. As the centuries passed, these coastal cities, especially Cerveteri (the ancient Caere) and Tarquinia suffered sporadic attacks from pirates and other marauders. When the Romans conquered Central Etruria and let her drainage system fall into ruins, malaria took further toll of the already reduced population.

Inland, many cities had been built on windy, isolated hills, Perugia, for a special example. From Perugia, you look down upon the Umbrian plain, more than a thousand feet below. Protected by her stone walls, Perugia held out stoutly against Rome until starvation and threatened fire made her surrender. Perugia's policy of expansion had at last become unendurable to the ambitious young city on the Tiber.

7

To reach Perugia, the Romans had had to make their way through dark, forbidding mountain country, but they had pressed on, regardless of lurking beasts and desperate fighting-men until at last they breached the thick stone walls and entered the city.

No great mounds are to be seen around the countryside here; for Perugia's noble families, by carving their handsome tombs out of the rocky hillsides, developed a new type of funerary architecture. Today family after family have lost the privacy of their rock-cut tombs; now their burial-urns are exposed to view in the National Museum of Perugia. But the families are still together, each member's ash enclosed in his urn.

Ancient Etruscan Veii, closer to Rome and a greater threat than Perugia to Rome's growing economy, was also built on a hill. The fate of Veii is often thought of as a symbol of Rome's implacable hatred. Known throughout the Mediterranean world for her stout-hearted citizens, her wealth, and her artistic ability, Veii fought fourteen wars with Rome before a trick brought her to destruction. Today, the wedge-shaped promontory where the proud city-state of Veii once stood is only a dreary waste.

Yet Veii had been a prosperous city, living from agriculture, handicraft, and metal-working. She had incurred Rome's animosity by refusing to surrender her salt-works near the mouth of the Tiber River. Her prosperity as early as the seventh century B.C. is indicated, in part, by the size of her grave-mounds and by the grandeur of the tombs that have been found within them. The Grotta Campana, a tomb on the outskirts of the city, dated in the second half of the century, contained one of the earliest painted chamber tombs of Etruria. Archaeologists consider the Grotta Campana almost the equal of the famous painted tombs of Tarquinia.

The coast city of Cerveteri, farther from Rome than Veii, the Etruscans had also built upon a rocky hill and fortified with strong walls. Once Cerveteri covered over four hundred acres. On an elevation across the intervening valley, eighty-seven acres were devoted to the necropolis where people took the deceased members of their families. Here countless great mounds rose, some as high as sixty feet. Now most of them have been leveled, their tombs only empty shells, attractions for tourists. Rock-girdled at the base, softly rounded above, the mounds of Cerveteri have kept their secrets over the centuries. Today, if it is spring when you walk along the "dead highway," the grass-grown street bordered by the locked underground tombs, the roadsides will be pink with blooming asphodel, the flower the ancients associated with death. Here ruts made long ago by the death-carriages are still visible, as are the small pillars and imitation houses that stand before many of the tombs and that some believe symbolize procreation and fruition. Woman's place is in the house, and so an imitation house marks a woman's resting-place; man is the pillar of the house, and so his symbol is the pillar, or *phallus,* as some interpret the symbol.

Before the archaeologists discovered the secret of the mounds in Etruria, our only knowledge of the people who called themselves Rasenna came from the scanty notices of Greek and Roman antiquarians and historians. Their reiterated statements were doubted, though without justification, for it has become increasingly evident, from the archaeological study of the mounds, that Rome owed much of her own artistic and scientific achievement to what has come down to her from the people she knew as Etruscans. Today their rock-girdled mounds, their roads, sewers, and tunnels still stand in Italy as monuments to the technical skill of builders who lived some two thousand years ago.

Their jewelry of beaten gold, which recalls to many enthusiasts the early Cretan goldwork, their vases, their bronzes, even their household utensils, and especially their wall-paintings (so like those in Egyptian tombs) all reveal a high level of artistic craftsmanship unequaled by any contemporary people of antiquity except the Greeks.

If the Etruscans once lived in Lydia, we should not be surprised to hear that they had cunning fingers when they worked with gold. Even so, they could not equal Lydia's mythical king, Midas, whose fingers turned to gold everything they touched.

In the early days of the Roman Empire recognition of these mysterious people who had overrun almost the whole of Italy and who had ruled Rome herself for many decades rose high enough for men of rank to begin claiming Etruscan descent. Because he was a scion of the old Etruscan aristocracy, Maecenas, the patron and friend of the Roman poet, Virgil, refused to accept a title from Rome's new ruler, Octavian. Virgil also claimed Etruscan descent, on his mother's side, and more than one critic has thought that he may have owed something of his poet's imagination to his mother's family. Born in the first century B.C. on a farm near Mantua, the former capital of the Northern Confederation of Etruria, where even in his day the Etruscans played a leading rôle, Virgil perhaps came into contact with many others who also claimed Etruscan ancestry.

Later on, when the Roman Empire had enemies to face who were more of a threat to her existence than the Etruscans had ever been, interest in the past languished or was confined at most to the antiquarians. Then for centuries the huge mounds remained the undisturbed feeding-places of sheep and goats, or occasionally provided a peasant farmer with new land to be had in return for plowing up its rich soil.

By the fifteenth century of our era many a famous old city had utterly lost its name, though tales of a glorious past still lingered. Little by little the tales included mention of strange weapons or dirt-encrusted jewels picked up around the countryside. It is easy to imagine that often a passerby might discover the partly choked entrance to one of the mounds and venturing within find himself in an underground chamber built of stone, with decorated pillars, and strange paintings on the walls, but with no sign of life except perhaps a snake or bat, or other creatures of the dark. Though the archaeologists have penetrated the secrets of the mounds and have learned, as George Dennis writes, all the details of Etruscan life, "from the cradle to the grave," they have not answered the question so often asked, why the Etruscans built these huge mounds. Speculation runs in two directions: that they wanted to prove to themselves and to the rest of the Mediterranean world that they had achieved the material recognition they had sought; or that they were motivated, quite simply and single-mindedly, by a spiritual concept, their extraordinary concept of the After Life, in which they would be revered as ancestral gods.

In 1864, Fustel de Coulanges, a professor of history at Strasbourg, published *La Cité Antique,* afterward reprinted several times and in 1873 translated into English. Beneath the surface of Greek and Latin classical writings, de Coulanges found a primitive world entirely dominated by religion. To this primitive world, he feels that the ancient Etruscans belonged.

The ancient Hindu world, de Coulanges also noted, was equally dominated by religion; in this world he saw analogies with the Hebrew and with the Etruscan primitive worlds, and particularly with the Etruscan. To de Coulanges, the Hindus, the early Greeks and Romans, and the Etruscans sprang from the same stratum of primitive civilization. This stratum historians designate as pre-Indo-European, pre-Germanic, or pre-Aegean. De Coulanges finds in this primitive world almost identical ideas relating to the four most important aspects of human existence: birth, death, burial, and a second life of the soul.

In 1878, George Dennis, for some years a British consul in Italy, produced his illuminating book: *The Cities and Cemeteries of Etruria.* Dennis, who supports the view of Herodotus that the Etruscans came from Anatolia, points out a similarity between the Etruscan and the Hebrew cosmogonies: in the Etruscan cosmogony preserved by the Greek lexicographer Suidas a creator spent twelve thousand years fashioning the world and its creatures; in the Hebrew cosmogony a creator spent six days, and rested on the seventh. The times differ greatly, the point is that in each a creator is at work.

Condensed and paraphrased, Dennis's account of the Etruscan cosmogony runs as follows: in the first two thousand years the creator made heaven and earth; in the second the apparent firmament; in the third the sea and all other waters; in the fourth the great lights—the sun, the moon, and the stars; in the fifth the birds, the reptiles, and the four-footed animals; and in the sixth two thousand years he made man.

De Coulanges, fourteen years later, did not mention a cosmogony; evidently to him this primitive stratum had no conception of a creator; it could not, therefore, have evolved a cosmogony. Neither the Greek Zeus, nor the Hebrew Jahweh, nor the Roman Jupiter, nor the Etruscan Tinia had been conceived of. Many a century had to pass before Tinia, afterward equated with Jupiter, became the creator of all things.

For no cosmogony could have been built upon the only gods these people knew, their deified ancestors who lived under the hearthstone and demanded constant tendance. Later, when other modes of burial were devised, the great mounds arose to protect the ancestors in the period when their hold on life was so tenuous before they entered into their second life.

II

MI LARTHIA

From the darkness of a grass-covered mound situated not far from Cerveteri, there came to light one April day in 1836 some of the most beautiful jewelry the world has ever seen. The story of its discovery and of the royal tomb in which it was found is one of the more romantic episodes of nineteenth-century archaeology.

Though the first quarter of the nineteenth century saw the beginning of scientific investigation of Etruscan tombs in central Italy, much of the work that was undertaken was too hasty, and lacked the scientific safeguards of modern archaeology. This was particularly true when several of the wealthy landowners near Cerveteri, some through interest, some through greed, became amateur archaeologists.

One of these interested explorers was Lucien Bonaparte, Prince of Canino, who owned a large tract of land near Vulci, the modern Volci, situated beyond Tarquinia, on the banks of the Fiora River. In the vicinity of prosperous Vulci, many Etruscan tombs were opened before the famous royal tomb near Cerveteri was discovered, that auspicious April day in 1836.

Eight years before, a peasant, while plowing on Lucien Bonaparte's land near Vulci, was astounded when the ground suddenly gave way under the feet of his ox, or oxen. The peasant, investigating, saw that he had broken through what appeared to be some kind of stonework.

A few days later, Lucien Bonaparte found that the stonework was the ceiling of an Etruscan tomb. Under his direction, the tomb was opened and its treasures of gold jewelry, bronzes, vases, and funerary equipment carried away to a place of safety.

During the next four months from a small plot of ground only three or four acres in extent, Lucien Bonaparte dug up more than two thousand authentic Etruscan pieces. From then on he became an ardent collector, and his wife as eager as he.

Inspired by his success, other wealthy landowners followed the prince's example and began to dig on their own properties. The next two years saw hundreds of tombs opened and thousands of Etruscan objects removed. Many, in the years to come, were to form the basis of large private collections; others found their way, eventually, into the various museums of Europe and America.

In 1836, two Italians, General Galassi, whose name now stands on a shop front in Florence, and a priest, Regulini, approached Lucien Bonaparte for permission to excavate a mound on his property near Cerveteri. The mound lay a little distance from Cerveteri, where, since then, a great archaic burial-ground has been excavated.

When the two Italians had secured permission from Lucien Bonaparte (though it is true that some authorities say the land belonged to Regulini), they hired several strong-armed fellows, provided them with picks and shovels, and late in April, Regulini and Galassi arrived at the mound.

The mound was dome-shaped and not particularly large. Early travelers in Italy have reported seeing mounds at least a hundred feet in diameter, and sixty feet or so in height. Since then, agricultural needs and haphazard attempts at excavation have reduced these large mounds and many others to lesser proportions.

Accounts of the opening of the mound vary. One account states that the two explorers found the entrance to the corridor and had it cleared out so that they could go in.

The other account, if less accurate, is more dramatic. The peasants, starting at the top of the grass-covered mound, had not dug far before they struck stone which proved to be the ceiling of the tomb. Fearful of what they might find within, the diggers wanted to stop. Finally they were persuaded to make an opening. They dropped flares through; then one by one, they followed the flares down into the dim interior.

Regulini and Galassi dropped down behind their men, who were standing, panic-stricken, almost directly underneath the gaping hole in the roof of the mound. Re-assured by the arrival of their employers, the men went on, if reluctantly. Soon the explorers found themselves in a long, narrow corridor that led to a vaulted gallery with a coffered ceiling. Along one wall, war-shields were painted; against the opposite wall, bronze shields leaned.

In the center of the gallery stood a bronze bed with a curved and decorated bronze headpiece. The bed was empty, but fiber scraps seemed to show that it had once held a mattress. (Apparently Regulini and Galassi did not notice the fragments of bone that the English traveler, Mrs. Hamilton Gray, reports having seen on the bronze bed when, three years later, in 1839, she visited ancient Etruria.)

Ranged along the side of the bed opposite the bronze shields, the intruders saw a row of small earthenware figures. Near by were an incense-burner and some silver bowls. The priest, Regulini, thought the small figures might represent Etruscan deities to whom the occupant of the tomb had been accustomed to sacrifice.

Up-ended against the wall on either side of the entrance were two bronze and wood vehicles with bronze fittings and high wheels. One was four-wheeled and had a long, flat body. The other, though partly broken and charred as if it had been exposed to fire, had obviously been a war-chariot, as its long tongue indicated.

The presence of the four-wheeled vehicle was easily understood; its length and breadth exactly matched the length and breadth of the bronze bed—an Etruscan hearse, no doubt, and used to bring the dead man to his new home.

The presence of the war-chariot had puzzled Regulini and Galassi until they found in another chamber a cremation-urn, obviously that of a warrior, because of his funeral gifts: a spear, a helmet, and pieces of armor. Scholars now think that the chariot in the first chamber belonged to the warrior, that it had probably been only partially consumed on his funeral pyre, and had then been brought to the mound, that, according to Etruscan belief, he might use it in his next life. Why it had not been left in the warrior's own chamber is unexplained.

Returning to the first chamber, Regulini and Galassi noticed what they had overlooked before, at the rear a partition and a door.

Some accounts add that when Regulini and Galassi opened the communicating door and stepped inside, their torches flashed on gold and jewels everywhere. They began to scoop up the treasure, and then saw that the jewels outlined the form of a human being, long since fallen into dust.

Resplendent in its shroud of gold, wearing a rarely beautiful headdress and a gold pectoral, adorned with necklaces and bracelets of beaten gold, finger rings and earrings set with precious stones, the body had been brought, centuries ago, to dwell in state in its underground home.

Here, according to Etruscan belief, both body and soul would continue to live secure and happy, as long as the members of its family above ground remembered to bring to the tomb the food and drink, especially the blood needed to sustain its frail and tenuous existence.

Cupidity overcame scruples. Regulini and Galassi and their men hastily gathered together everything they could find. The treasure amounted to more than six hundred and fifty pieces. The tomb furniture, apparently, they did not then disturb.

Since at that time Cerveteri (Caere) lay within the Papal dominions, the contents of the tomb were eventually brought to the Vatican. Now everything from the Regulini-Galassi tomb is in the

Gregorian Museum of the Vatican. Among the jewels there are a large gold pectoral, and a strangely beautiful gold *fibula*, or brooch, ovoid in shape. Gold earrings are there, too, a pair of massive bracelets of gold filigree work, necklaces, rings, and minute fragments of gold, possibly from a gold shroud.

The inventory that was finally made of the treasure from the Regulini-Galassi tomb included six silver goblets of beautiful design and workmanship, made either in Greece or by a Greek artist in Etruria, the experts say, and inscribed with two words in Etruscan characters. Mrs. Hamilton Gray, who published in 1840 as faithful an account as she could recall of her Etruscan visit, says she saw three of these silver goblets in a private collection in Italy. But at that time she did not know what the words meant.

Just three years before the mound was entered, a twenty-three-year-old German Egyptologist, Richard Lepsius, added the finishing touch to research into the phonetic values of Etruscan characters by determining the value of a letter that had not been previously identified. Since then Etruscologists have been able to transliterate into their Latin equivalents almost all the Etruscan inscriptions that have come to light. They have not yet been able to agree upon the identification of many individual words nor upon their meanings.

The two words that Mrs. Gray had seen on the silver goblets were written, after the Etruscan fashion, from right to left. Reversed and transliterated the words are:

MI LARTHIA

Though history knows of no woman by this name, Larthia has done her best to reach us by having her silver cups inscribed: *I am Larthia,* sending her name down from the seventh century B.C. For the archaeologists have decided that the resplendent tomb—usually called the "royal tomb"—with its private burial chamber belongs to the first half of the seventh century.

Larthia had her jewel box with her, and in it were other treasures: rings, amber pendants set in gold, armlets, earrings, and gold spirals she may have worn in her hair. Near where her feet had once rested were ornaments of gold, shaped like lotus blossoms, perhaps worn on gilded sandals.

Three years after the opening of the Regulini-Galassi tomb, the Princess of Canino appeared at an ambassadorial party wearing a large gold pectoral on her breast that made her the envy of every woman present. Soon a whisper made the rounds of society, that the gold pectoral had come from the tomb Regulini and Galassi had opened.

Today, the gold *fibula,* the gold pectoral, and other magnificent pieces of jewelry may be seen in the Gregorian Museum of the Vatican. Scarcely a day passes without its throng of visitors crowding around the tall glass case to admire the jewelry from the Regulini-Galassi tomb.

No one really knows who the dead lady in the private chamber was. Some disregard the apparently feminine name on the silver cups and consider that such massive gold jewelry must have belonged to a high priest, or to some man of rank. Von Vacano (*The Etruscans in the Ancient World*) and others accept the name and the woman Larthia. He believes she may have been a queen of Cerveteri, for in the seventh century B.C. certain city-states were probably ruled by kings. And since to be a woman in Etruscan days meant far more than it ever did to either the Greeks or the Romans, it is not necessarily too far-fetched to see the Lady Larthia as a queen who merits a splendid tomb.

The ovoid-shaped *fibula* is not the ordinary kind of ancient shoulder pin, but a large clasp in two parts, originally hinged together; as restored in the museum, rigid, the reconstructed hinge making its overall height about twelve and a half inches.

The upper part of the *fibula* is decorated in relief with two bands of intertwined flowers, separated by a plain strip. The inner band encloses five lions, two above and three below.

The lower part, made smaller to fit beneath the upper, is convex, to protect the fastening pin. This part, though not visible when the *fibula* was worn, is nevertheless decorated with seven rows of ducks, each row separated from the next by incredibly small lions,

18

also in relief. The whole is a beautiful and intricate specimen of the jeweler's craftsmanship.

Von Vacano thinks that both the gold pectoral and the *fibula* were signs of rank; Larthia, he suggests, may have worn the gold pectoral on her breast and on ceremonial occasions the *fibula* as part of an ornamental headdress. (He also suggests that the occupant of the chamber with the bronze bed may have been Larthia's son, or possibly her husband.)

The pectoral, sixteen and a half inches long and almost as broad, is made of gold foil. Originally it may have been backed with thin sheet copper, since traces of copper were still to be seen, von Vacano says, when the pectoral was first examined. The gold foil is embossed with twelve bands of minute figures: sphinxes, goats, winged horses and demons, panthers and deer. The bands are separated by lines of little bosses punched in such a way as to give the effect of strings of beads.

Similar breastplates have been found elsewhere, von Vacano reports. He feels that such elaborate gold breast coverings "have their place in the series of jewels from which emanated religious power and the splendour of authority in the same way as the Golden Fleece and the shield of Athena."

By way of comparison, von Vacano cites a gold breastplate from the Bocchoris tomb near Tarquinia, which was found with the remains of a woman who was buried there. The breastplate was of "gold foil richly decorated in orientalizing style." He also cites an Oriental bronze bowl in the British Museum and an amber statuette in the Museum of Fine Arts in Boston. The design on the bronze bowl shows a winged sphinx running ahead of the "swiftly travelling hunting chariot of the king. The sphinx is wearing a *bib* which in shape and in size is very similar to that worn by the dead woman in the Regulini-Galassi tomb." The amber statuette in the Museum of Fine Arts in Boston depicts the "Assyrian King Ashurnasir-pal as a royal priest," wearing a breastplate divided into panels and decorated with rosettes.

Centuries ago, the fabulous pectoral from the Regulini-Galassi tomb, with its matching earrings and bracelets, may have been worn in a far different setting, not by Larthia a Queen, but by Larthia, a beautiful Etruscan lady. Nor would she have been at a gala evening in an Embassy, but at an Etruscan banquet. Here the ladies, attired in their best, reclined on soft cushions beside their gentlemen, with acrobats and dancing-girls to entertain them while they dined, perhaps on roast duck stuffed with water-chestnuts and washed down with good Etruscan wine.

If Larthia was a queen of Cerveteri, then the distinguished person in the first chamber may, von Vacano suggests, have been Larthia's son. That he was Larthia's husband is doubtful, unless this burial is a departure from the usual Etruscan custom of interring a married couple beside each other, as the arrangement of the sculptured effigies on many a sarcophagus indicates.

Though the Lady Larthia and her jewels were not discovered until after the middle of the nineteenth century, in 1498 a Dominican monk of Viterbo published a detailed account of the contents of several Etruscan tombs. Excited artists and poets flocked to see the treasures; among them was Michelangelo, who is said to have sketched the head of the Etruscan king of the underworld. Unaware or not of this tradition from the Italian Renaissance, some critics see Etruscan influence in *The Last Judgement;* they say that the Greek Charon, the ferryman of the dead, resembles the Etruscan Charun, the king of the underworld.

As the years wheeled by, more mounds were uncovered, and more magnificent treasures came to light, treasures that centuries ago, long before the birth of Christ, loving hands had carried into the homes of the dead that their occupants might not lack for comfort and enjoyment in the shadowy life of the tomb.

From the shadows of her tomb the voice of the Lady Larthia has spoken clearly to us: MI LARTHIA, she says. But hers is only one voice from the past, and we need the help of other voices from other tombs before we can feel that we are beginning to learn what the mental and spiritual qualities of the Etruscan mind were that led to the downfall of these talented people at the hands of Rome.

III

The Homes of the Dead

Larthia's seventh-century tomb was unlike those of earlier days the Etruscans built to accommodate the departed members of their families. Hers was a chambered tomb, probably modeled upon her own Etruscan house. Some archaeologists think that this final home of Larthia's had originally been intended for her alone, and later enlarged to accommodate others of her family.

The chamber Larthia and her jewels were found in may at first have been a narrow trench, cut out of tufa, the yellowish stone formed of baked volcanic soil that yields easily to cutting tools. Then, later, the trench would have been made into a chamber, with perhaps a shelf to serve as a bier; and blocks of the same tufa added to increase the height of the walls; and finally, two more chambers were hollowed out. More blocks of the same tufa were arranged in narrowing circles overhead until the opening at the top became small enough to be closed with a single flat slab. A girdle of stone at its base and earth mounded high above completed the dwelling where Larthia and her two companions were to await the day of their deliverance from the abyss of the underworld. For, during the seventh century B.C. the Etruscans seem still to have believed that they would spend at least a part of their second life in a subterranean world.

Some authorities say that the Tyrrhenians introduced into Italy the corbel, or so-called false vaulting, formed by continuous courses of stone. A reconstruction of a sixth-century tomb with the false vaulting may be seen in the garden of the Archaeological Museum at Florence. This tomb is inscribed in Etruscan characters as Larthia's silver goblets were. *Mi Velthurus,* the inscription reads; the name is that of a family who lived near Orvieto in central Etruria.

The mound with its girdle of stone at the base may have originated from the earlier practice of burying individual members of a family in separate graves and then setting up around them a circle of stone slabs. To protect the graves, earth was then heaped up within the stone circle. And gradually, as the years passed, the mounds became higher and higher.

Since these graves were usually family tombs, it became necessary, as the family increased in size, to fashion an entrance. Then a passage was cut through the stonework at the base, giving rise to a corridor-tomb like Larthia's.

As the centuries passed and populations increased, the building of huge mounds had to be limited to the amount of level ground available, and crowding became inevitable. In cliff country, rock-cut tombs were the solution. Often tomb-makers burrowed deep down into the rock. To reach chambers so far beneath the surface long flights of steps had to be cut. Many of the tombs that visitors to Tarquinia wish to see have entrances so frighteningly steep that women in high-heeled shoes refuse to risk going down them, and thus miss seeing these many-chambered homes of the dead.

Some of these tombs have waist-high biers that have been cut out of the rock. On these biers the dead were laid out. You can still see the ridges that mark off the individual spaces. On the men's side, the spaces are long enough and wide enough to accommodate a full grown man; on the women's side the spaces are shorter and narrower. Occasionally a woman's bier is at the foot of a man's. The size of the chamber seems to be the determining factor.

Common people were either cremated and placed in burial-urns or well-wrapped and enclosed in wooden coffins, then put into pits or trenches and decently covered over. Etruscan slaves were decently buried, too, as members of the family. They were not tossed into a great common pit, and left there for the birds and dogs to dispose of as Roman slaves were. They were cremated and their urns placed in small graves dug out of the sides of the mound.

Children were never cremated, nor were they, as a rule, buried with the family. In the necropolis at Cerveteri a child's stone coffin, with the skeleton, was found outside the tomb, its small possessions intact.

Exceptions occur, though. When one tomb at Cerveteri was opened, a stone bier had been prepared for a woman's body. Her stone pillow had been hollowed out for her head; and alongside there was a shallow depression, just the right size for a baby's head. Perhaps a small infant could not be separated from its mother.

There is no evidence, as yet, that infants were buried under the floor of the family house, a custom prevalent in some early cultures, to enable the spirit of the dead infant to return in the person of the next child to be born. Though children were not cremated, the discovery of a cremation-urn in the warrior's chamber of the Regulini-Galassi tomb and of the bronze bed with, apparently, fragments of uncharred bone offers evidence that both forms of burial existed at the same time. One's chance of a second life could not, therefore, have been dependent upon the form of burial.

Today the bronze bed, the four-wheeled car, and the chariot, but not the cremation-urn, are all in the same room of the Gregorian Museum in the Vatican.

The bronze bed with its curved headpiece is particularly interesting. Its frame rests on six pillar-like legs, each rounded off at the top and tapering below. Metal strips, also of bronze, criss-cross each other to form a stout lattice support. The remnants of fiber that Mrs. Gray saw may mean that a mattress was placed upon the lattice work. Illustrations on several funerary urns show that the Etruscans did use mattresses on their beds.

The chariot of wood and bronze is as interesting as the bed; its long, slender bronze tongue, facing you as you enter the museum, indicates that it was drawn by two horses. A lion's head, exquisitely carved, decorates the end of the tongue. Since the chariot shows signs of having been partially burned, perhaps on the funeral pyre, that its owner, the warrior, might use it in his new life beyond the grave, doubtless his horses had also been burned on the pyre, for without horses the chariot would be useless to him.

If the warrior was one of Larthia's attendants, he may have been slain that his shade might continue serving her in the After World. Then he would have gone to his pyre, riding triumphantly in his chariot.

Some Etruscan reliefs on tombstones and elsewhere show deceased persons traveling on foot to the After World; others ride in carriages, or on horseback. This should mean that their horses had been cremated, that their shades could also be used in the After World.

As every anthropologist knows, the horse is a chthonian animal, that is, an animal dedicated to the lower world. As a chthonian animal, the horse played its part in the funeral ceremonial of ancient Greece. That dramatic part the horse still retains. With stirrups reversed, carrying its dead master's equipment, the general's horse, or the king's, is led in the funeral procession, a folk-rite left from the days when a man's horse was led to his grave to be sacrificed.

An Etruscan funeral procession, with the mourners carrying white, black, and purple figs, is portrayed on a cup in the Vatican. The artist has chosen the moment when the procession is leaving the city gate. Two mules draw the funeral carriage; beside it walk two men, heralds perhaps. On the carriage lies the body of a bearded man. His head is adorned with ornaments, his body covered with a cloak.

Two persons are seated beside the dead man: one a young woman, the other a young man. Behind the two young people an older man is seated. Musicians playing on the double flute precede the cortege; armed soldiers, heads bent, spears reversed, follow.

The soldiers' shields carry devices of various kinds; they may represent different companies or regiments, whose leaders have sent delegations to honor the dead man, perhaps a nobleman, or other man of rank. Just such a funeral procession as this Larthia's son may have had.

All the furnishings essential for a nobleman's life in the After World were brought and placed in his tomb. Among the contents from the Regulini-Galassi tomb in the Gregorian Museum are two huge bronze cauldrons almost six feet in circumference. Each cauldron is ornamented with five lions' heads, turned so that they look outwards. From other tombs have come platters, bowls, fire dogs, grates, a low four-wheeled tray, apparently an incense-burner, stools, tables, candelabra, everything that a nobleman has been accustomed to in the house of wood he has now exchanged for this lasting home of stone. Here he will welcome his friends and relatives when they come bringing him the food and drink which he needs to sustain the frail flickering life he must lead in his tomb until the day of his release.

One of the furnishings of the Regulini-Galassi tomb was a large, throne-like chair with a foot stool attached. The centuries had treated the chair badly, its wooden frame worst of all, but the bronze sheathing over the wood had preserved its shape. It has been carefully reconstructed but you must imagine for yourself how its shining bronze must once have glittered, since a dark green patina has now overspread the bronze.

Von Vacano has described the chair as follows: "Rich beaten work, prancing lions and stags and plants in the orientalizing style, decorate the top of the back rest and the box-shaped support of the seat. The two front legs curving slightly inwards terminate in animal feet. Right and left horse busts spring from the front edge of the seat, and small arm-rests both end in bronze boxes, each decorated with a sculptured poppy head. The rectangular space between the boards which frame the back rest would have been upholstered with fabric or leather, as would the seat." The famous Corsini chair of marble in the Villa Giulia in Rome that always attracts the attention of visitors has no foot stool, but two impressive arm chairs in the seventh-century Tomb of Shields and Chairs in Tarquinia have foot stools attached.

Arm chairs such as these, von Vacano suggests, may have formed a part of Etruscan funeral ceremonies, especially ceremonies for persons of rank. But such a chair might easily have been the chair of the master of the house, like the sofa in a middle class German home. Even an ordinary chair, though, must have had some significance, for burial-jars were often placed in round chairs which were then put carefully into the graves, to be discovered and wondered at thousands of years later.

In addition to the actual furniture that was placed in a tomb, painted semblances of chairs, tables, and other furniture are represented on ceilings, on pillars, and on walls. Even simulated doors and windows appear. Such representations fascinate the visitor today both for their decorative interest and for the story they tell of a way of life long past. But to the Etruscan they were no mere details of a life-story and no mere decoration. They were vital magic. By a kind of thinking the modern mind finds difficult to comprehend, the objects represented in the tombs could translate themselves into similar objects in the After World.

The simple magic they perform for us is especially notable when we look at the stucco reliefs on the pillars of the celebrated Tomb of the Reliefs in the necropolis at Cerveteri.

Easily recognized and identified as helmets, throwing-sticks, swords, pots and pans, a saw, coils of rope, a dog at the base of one pillar, an unidentified animal at the base of another, these take us back through the centuries and let us see the Etruscans as living, breathing people.

The impression is heightened if one visits the Tomb of the Little House, or Cottage, as it is often called. The Cottage has six small rooms opening one into the other. Each room contains stone benches. With mattresses spread upon the benches and chairs conveniently near, this Cottage near Cerveteri would make a charming home for an Etruscan family.

By contrast, the Campana Tomb seems a mansion. This tomb is in a large cemetery on a hill near Cerveteri, with a magnificent view of the valley beyond. The interior consists of a spacious central room, entered through arched doorways and opening into a corridor. At the end of the corridor is the principal chamber, flanked by two smaller ones.

The antechamber through which one passes to the principal chamber has a ceiling painted to imitate a semi-circular roof with radiating lines that seem to be rays of light. Two wooden chairs are also painted on the ceiling.

For a different kind of decoration, one must turn to the Painted Tombs of Tarquinia. On the walls of these underground chambers, painted in gay colors, groups of banqueters, men and women, recline on dining couches. They are served with food by naked slave boys, and entertained by dancers—young girls in transparent dresses and handsome youths in brightly-colored cloaks who play on flutes as they dance.

Some scenes are derived from Greek mythology, for as early as the sixth century B.C. the influence of Greece was felt in Etruria. Greek vases were being brought in by Etruscan navigators or by foreign traders who exchanged them for what the coastal cities had to offer. Even so, though the native artists may have been influenced by outsiders, their wall-paintings are never slavish copies; they show spirit and a verve truly Etruscan.

As in Egypt and in Crete the colors used in wall-paintings were relatively few, black, obtained from soot or charcoal; white, from chalk; red and pink derived from oxide. Later there were added yellow, from ochre; blue, obtained from the dust of lapis lazuli or from an artificial composition of copper, calcium, and flint; green, from malachite. The experts tell us that the plaster spread on the tufa walls consisted of a mixture of calcium carbonate and clay. Sometimes a little turf was added to keep the plaster from hardening before the artist was ready to apply his colors.

The composition of the mixture was discovered when, because of water seepage, it became necessary to remove the paintings from the walls of some of the tombs. This was a most delicate procedure; it involved saturating a double layer of fine linen in colorless shellac diluted with alcohol and applying the saturated linen to the painted surfaces. When the linen was pulled away, the painted plaster came off with it, unharmed. The detached paintings were then transferred to another double cloth impregnated with calcium caseate. Attached to adjustable rods, the painting was then set in a frame made of pine wood.

By this process the paintings from three of the tombs in Tarquinia—the Tomb of the Chariots, the Tomb of the Triclinium, and the Tomb of the Funeral Beds—have been transferred to the Etruscan Museum in the former Vitelleschi palace.

Furnished so amply with thoughtful concern for the needs of their waiting occupants, painted and decorated with Etruscan skill in the warm Etruscan colors, these tombs—thousands of them— have survived the centuries to reveal with surprising clarity the looks and ways of a vanished people. The revelation is incomplete, certainly. We are charmed almost magically into a momentary illusion that we understand these newly-found Etruscans, because the things they used and enjoyed have been so fully shown to us. But what the tombs most vitally meant to their creators, their magical assurance of life in an endless hereafter, when their familiar possessions would regain their usefulness in a continuance of the familiar world, that we cannot truly understand. Perhaps the great sarcophagi will afford a deeper penetration into the Etruscan vision of the After Life.

IV

The Great Sarcophagi
of the Nobles

The great sarcophagi, generally more than life-size, were the carved and painted coffins of the Etruscan nobles. Some are almost seven feet long and proportionally wide. They are made of terra-cotta or of stone, or occasionally of marble or alabaster or *nenfro*, a dark gray stone with a peculiar and rather unpleasant odor. To see these sarcophagi, one must go to the museums, because only a few remain in the tombs. The museums acquired them long ago.

An exception is the Tomb of the Sarcophagi, on the way to the necropolis of Cerveteri. The tomb lies on a short side street, just before you reach the so-called Tomb of the Tarquins. Here three great sarcophagi of alabaster have been left in their original places on the stone biers cut for them. Two of the sarcophagi have recumbent male figures sculptured on their lids. Inscriptions in Etruscan letters tell us that the persons represented here belonged to the family *Apucu,* but I have been unable to learn anything more about them than that they once lived in ancient Caere.

The use of alabaster for these sarcophagi, however, and the recumbent figures afford us some information. To be able to choose alabaster rather than the less expensive terra-cotta or stone indicates that the family was prosperous. To have the figures sculptured in a recumbent attitude indicates that the family lived in a comparatively late period of Etruscan life, perhaps the fourth century B.C. when recumbent figures were becoming fashionable.

In ancient Etruria when a sculptor was commissioned to carve two figures on the same sarcophagus, he used the half-reclining type. The museums possess many such sarcophagi; usually the two figures are those of a man and a woman, the woman half-reclining in the man's arms. For scholars who interpret the figures as husband and wife, their affectionate pose signifies the Etruscan attitude toward the sacredness of the matrimonial bond.

Together in life, husband and wife now recline together on the lid of their sarcophagus, not as if sleeping their last sleep, but vigorously alive, gazing proudly out with wide-open eyes upon the world of today, the husband with his *patera,* or libation-vessel, the wife with her mirror. Cheerful and smiling, at least in the early days, before Etruria lost her place in the sunshine of Italy, they are ready to carry on into the After World the same pleasant, aristocratic life they have always led.

Sometimes neither *patera* nor mirror is represented. Both are copies, of course, when they appear on the sarcophagi, as faithful to the originals as the material of the sculptured effigies permits.

Present or absent, both *patera* and mirror are almost equally hard to explain or to understand. Some scholars say that the Etruscan *patera* is a vessel intended not to pour a libation, but to receive the blood-gift which the deceased person needs. Against this interpretation is the fact that no woman in Etruscan art, at least as far as I am aware, is ever portrayed holding a *patera,* and surely a woman is in as great need of the revivifying blood as a man is. Also, among the various household utensils real or represented in painting in the Etruscan tombs, no vessel bears any resemblance to a shallow saucer with a boss in the center. Nor are they to be seen in the museums.

30

To my knowledge, no one has offered any adequate explanation of the boss. Surely it could not have served as a handle. Whatever the explanation of the boss may be, the *patera* itself, when represented in a man's hand, must have been significant. In the early Indo-European stratum to which the Etruscans belonged only the male head of a family could pour a libation to his ancestral gods. If this stricture applied to later days and was one of the old ways the Etruscans clung to, the appearance of a *patera* in a man's hand and not in a woman's is understandable.

In the museum at Tarquinia there is a large sarcophagus, usually known as the Sarcophagus of the Magistrate, a late work, executed perhaps even after Etruria had been absorbed into Rome. The effigy on the lid portrays an elderly man, with a strong face and clear eyes, who holds in his hand, not a *patera*, but an open scroll. The heavy necklace that reaches to his chest, the ring on his finger, and the scroll in his hand symbolize his official status: perhaps he held a post in the new Roman administration of some Etruscan city.

There are other such instances where a substitution seems to have been made for the *patera*, as though the individual represented needed some other kind of identification. In Rome, in the National Museum of the Villa Giulia, where numerous sarcophagi with effigies on their lids are on exhibition, some male figures appear holding, not *pateras*, but mirrors—unless what seem to be mirrors are really *pateras*.

Throughout the ancient world there existed a belief that a reflection, wherever seen, in the shadow that attaches itself to a man's heels and that walks with him as he goes his way, in the clear water of a pool, or in the shining surface of a mirror, is his other self, the animating principle of his being, his *anima*, or soul. Since the Etruscans must have shared this belief, we should not be surprised to see, occasionally, a sarcophagus with the effigy of a man with a mirror in his hand. Nor should we be surprised that neither a man nor a woman is ever, to my knowledge, shown gazing at his own reflection, as might be expected if Etruscan mirrors served only cosmetic needs.

31

I venture to suggest that the presence of a mirror in the hand of an effigy may be for purposes of identification in the next world, and that its omission may indicate the loss of the old belief in reflections.

Etruscan mirrors were round, made of bronze, furnished with long tongue-like handles, highly polished on the inner, or concave side, and engraved, usually with mythological or religious scenes, on the outer side. Some fifteen hundred have already been found in the tombs and are now in present-day museums. The Archaeological Museum in Florence has a splendid collection. The copies of these bronze mirrors which sculptured women (and apparently an occasional man) hold in their hands are never engraved. This seems to be an additional indication that a mirror was treasured for other than cosmetic purposes.

In the National Museum in Naples, two noble Etruscan ladies may be seen, each half-reclining on the lid of her sarcophagus. So life-like and so comfortable do these ladies seem, even though their stone beds are not carved to fit their bodies as some lids are, that at first one does not notice that neither lady holds a mirror. Since these sarcophagi are of late date, perhaps a mirror no longer served a symbolic purpose.

Visitors seldom have an opportunity to ask questions about these sarcophagi, because just beyond them lie one of the chief treasures of the museum, the plastic relief of ancient Pompeii before its destruction in 79 A.D., and the guides are more interested in the relief than in effigies of Etruscan ladies, with or without mirrors sculptured on the lids of their sarcophagi.

The relief is really fascinating, particularly if one knows that Pompeii was once an Oscan settlement. Though some time during the seventh century B.C. the Etruscans took the city from the Oscans, the Oscan language long persisted as the city's third language. The other two were Greek and Latin. The relief shows that the most irregular streets were those near the Forum, and these are thought to have been the oldest. When in the first century B.C. Rome conquered Pompeii, she followed her usual custom of replacing the decimated population by colonies of her own people. To Pompeii were sent colonies of war veterans.

Among other interesting Etruscan relics in the same museum are a pair of forceps, discovered in the ruins of a surgeon's house, and a *groma,* or surveyor's plane-table, that came from the shop of a metal-worker. Both point to the high level of civilization the Etruscans had reached.

In Paris, at the Louvre, one of the most prized possessions is a great terra-cotta sarcophagus from Cerveteri, dated about 520 B.C. On its lid a husband and wife are represented. Nude to the waist, as was the custom for a male figure, the man's torso is well-muscled and vigorous. He reclines on his left arm, a plump terra-cotta cushion under his elbow, his right arm extended and resting lightly on his wife's right shoulder. She leans back against her husband. Her gown is of soft material, finished at the neck with a soft collar, rolled at the upper and lower edges.

Both husband and wife wear their hair long, his parted in the middle and hanging down his back; hers held in place by a closely-fitting cap. From the cap tight braids escape, two falling over each shoulder. Their faces are serenely happy. They are not looking at each other, but forward, posed as if waiting for the photographer to say "cheese," or whatever the Etruscan equivalent was for that useful word. Neither member of the pair holds either a *patera* or a mirror or any other identifying object. But, though the wife has no mirror in her hand, and her husband no saucer-like *patera,* their fingers (as restored) are so curved that they could originally have held either a mirror or a *patera.*

An aristocratic pair, one imagines, probably so well-known in their social circle that they needed nothing to identify either of them in the After World. Looking at them, one can easily believe that only the nobles had their effigies carved on the lids of the great sarcophagi, possibly from the seventh century on, while the poor had to be content with a cheaper form of burial.

The fourth century through the second is the period of the recumbent figure, whether male or female, which anticipates the outstretched form on the sarcophagi of the Middle Ages.

In the Archaeological Museum in Florence there is an alabaster sarcophagus of the fourth century. A woman with covered head is seated with her back supported against her husband's outstretched right arm. In his right hand he holds a *patera*. His wife has no mirror, as she might well have had, to admire the beautiful gold necklace she is wearing. Perhaps she is apprehensive because she has no mirror, or perhaps she prefers to remain unidentified in a second life which may only duplicate the unhappy period she is now passing through. For in the fourth century B.C. Etruria was no longer a great power.

A popular type of the period seems to be that of the *obesus Etruscus,* which many have accepted as typical of the Etruscan male. He is shown with a wrinkled face, heavy jowls, a soft body, and a protuberant belly, reclining on a cushion or mattress, with a goblet instead of a *patera* in his right hand. In him we see realism at its worst, and death shorn of all its dignity.

A sarcophagus of approximately the same period, now in the basement of the British Museum, shows the recumbent figure of a woman. Nestled close beside her is the tender, delicate figure of a young wild creature, a fawn perhaps, going with her to the After World. Her face has the serenity of an earlier age.

Apparently there was no rigid custom sculptors had to follow in making funeral statuary. Some scholars have suggested that shops kept in stock what the trade required, or fashion demanded, in the way of sculptured sarcophagi and funerary urns, and that when the proper time came, the customer's own head was modeled and attached to whatever torso or full length figure he desired. The aristocratic nobleman probably ordered what suited his pleasure, much as people do today when they select, in advance, the kind of coffin they wish to be buried in.

Would any nobleman have pushed realism to such an extent as to select for himself an *obesus Etruscus?*

These same centuries in Etruria seem to have ushered in the custom of using the sides of the great sarcophagi for scenes in bas-relief. The preferred scenes are those from Greek mythology, or, as pessimism crept into the Etruscan soul, dreadful pictures of life in the After World.

An unusually large third-century sarcophagus in the museum at Orvieto, nearly seven feet long and over two and a half feet wide, represents an episode from the *Odyssey*. The artist has chosen the scene where the hero Odysseus, sword in hand, threatens Circe with death unless she releases his men from the beast-forms she has turned them into. Two unfortunate wretches, half-beast, half-man, await their freedom.

The Archaeological Museum in Florence contains a few sar-cophagi of the fourth century made of the dark gray *nenfro*. On the lid of one of these sarcophagi the recumbent figure of a thickset man is portrayed. There is nothing striking about him. Indeed, one would pass him by, were it not that a bas-relief on one side of his sarcophagus shows a husband and wife playing a game of *kottábos*.

That the game is being played in the After World is indicated by the presence of a winged *Lasa*, an Etruscan goddess of death.

Kottábos was a game the Etruscan élite indulged in at banquets. The game was played by two persons seated, or reclining, on the same dining-couch. In front of the couch an attendant places a tall bronze standard with several arms, each arm terminating in a small bronze cup. Each player in turn tries to flip drops of wine from his goblet into a cup. The winner was probably the person who first succeeded in flipping wine into a whole set of cups. Some of the standards in Florence are five or six feet high, with a half-dozen or so cups. How close the standards stood to the dining-couch we do not know, nor whether the attendant moved them to bring the empty cups closer to the player.

In this scene husband and wife are obviously enjoying themselves with their favorite game. We see nothing frightening, nothing un-pleasant here. But horrifying scenes do occur in the fourth century, demons armed with bows and arrows conducting the souls of the dead to the After World, where they are handed to Tuchulcha to beat them to death with his huge club.

A hideous figure Tuchulcha is, conjured up by some one's distorted imagination, with snaky hair, hooked nose, the ears of a horse, and great curved wings. Wings imply flight. Flight implies the upper air. On the *nenfro* sarcophagus, the Etruscan goddess of death is also shown with wings. Yet we have no evidence that the Etruscans ever transferred their subterranean After World to the skies.

To preserve one's identity down in the After World played an important part in Etruscan religious belief. To carry a mirror in one's hand would help; but the reflection of one's self within the mirror was, at best, pale and blurred, and possibly untrue. Something more tangible was needed. The *patera* in the hand of an Etruscan man may have distinguished him as a *lucumo*, a priest-king, entitled to pour libations at a time of sacrifice, on the sacred feast-days in honor of the dead. To preserve his identity in the After World, the *lucumo* must carry with him the tangible sign of his religious office. This theory might mean that a man without a *patera* was not a *lucumo*, or priest-king.

The need to preserve one's identity is one of the reasons for placing beside a warrior's urn some distinguishing mark of his profession, his helmet or his spear. The problem of identification in the After World must have been even more troubling when household pots, jars, or other plain receptacles were used for burial purposes. To help solve the problem potters began to make urns, at first in rude semblances of the human body, with staring eyes and embryonic arms. To see these strange urns, we must look at what is called Villanovan pottery.

V

The Hermetic Urn

The Villanovans were an early Iron Age people in Italy, antedating the Etruscans, who cremated their dead, put the ashes into bi-conical, or double-coned, urns, and buried them in the ground.

Some one, with a singular lack of imagination, bestowed the name Villanovan upon these people merely because the first of their lost cemeteries was discovered near Villanova, a small village three miles north of Bologna. The strange bi-conical urns Count Gozzadi found in the cemetery, when he unearthed it in 1853, were assigned to the ninth and eighth centuries B.C.

Quantities of other urns, variously shaped, were also found. Each had been set upright in its own pit-grave, often two feet or so deep and about half as wide. Some were lined with small stones. In a few instances, several urns had been put into the same grave, placed one on top of the other.

The discovery of this Villanovan cemetery and of the others that followed has been valuable to the historian, the archaeologist, and the student of primitive religion. For the historian, the discovery was valuable because the Villanovans antedated the Etruscans, and study of their civilization has cast new light upon that of the Etruscans. For the archaeologist the discovery was even more valuable, because the increasing number of artifacts that came to light caused him to develop scientific methods of recording his finds.

The student of primitive religion also had much to learn from the size and shape of the burial-urns, from their decoration, and from the gifts that were found with them.

Fortunately burial-urns from many other places in Italy are now so numerous and so well displayed in most of our museums that they can be easily studied.

An average bi-conical urn of the early Villanovan type is between seventeen and eighteen inches high, of reddish or yellowish clay, according to the region where it has been made, and fired to a deeper shade. Both cones are decorated, usually with geometric or swastika designs. Each cone has a strong handle, sometimes plain, sometimes decorated. The upper, or inverted, cone is generally covered with a lid, which is often only a shallow saucer placed upside down.

On the lid of one bi-conical urn—of the Villanovan type—from an Etruscan cemetery near Volterra, a short distance southwest of Florence, a man is shown seated at a table with a large wine bowl in front of him. The scene has been interpreted as a banquet in the After World, at which the man is host. Near by stands a woman. She seems to be waiting for recognition. We may take it that the woman is the man's wife, just arrived from the upper world and expecting a welcome from her husband.

Perhaps on the original wine bowl the maker had written in Etruscan characters some such proverb as the following that Mayani has put together out of isolated words he has studied:

"Drink, to know a little joy,
And drink to live long."

Care seems to have been taken to gather up even the smallest fragments of bone from the funeral pyre and to place them with the ash in the burial-urn, where today exposed to the view of the curious they may still be seen, a melancholy sight.

Beside the urns in their pit-graves various identifying gifts were found: a knife, a necklace, a distaff, a horse's bit, a sword, a jug with a drinking cup. Occasionally, these gifts seem more delicately made than would be practicable for daily use, the walls of a cup too thin, a saucer too fragile. The value of a gift, however, was not what counted, but its usefulness in the After World, prompted, one would like to believe, by the loving thought of the giver. After all, the Etruscans were people like ourselves, and among them natural family feeling was strong.

Besides the bi-conical urns, other types have also been found in early burial-fields. Among these are canopic-urns, helmet-urns, and hut-urns.

The so-called canopic-urns are the ones that attract most visitors in the archaeological museums. The name comes from Canopus in Egypt, where the god Osiris was worshiped under the peculiar form of a vase with a human head. By a process mythologists call *contamination,* the name came to be applied to the Egyptian vases with human or animal heads in which, after a deceased person had been embalmed, his internal organs were placed.

In Etruria, many canopic burial-jars, with lids in the shape of a human head, round, often expressive eyes, rudimentary nose, and short arms that usually rest on a squat body, have been found in a limited area near Chiusi, which seems to have been a center for their manufacture. Some of these astonishing urn-figures (generally like the Villanovan urns between seventeen and eighteen inches high) wear large earrings; and a few have been found dressed as though they were dolls. The shape of the canopic-jars, the earrings, and the clothing create the feeling that a mysterious kind of alchemy may indeed be taking place within the squat urn-figure.

The resemblance to human beings is even more startling when we see canopic-urns seated on round chairs of bronze or terra-cotta. An especially dignified canopus from Solaia in central Etruria is seated in what appears to be an extraordinarily good copy of the modern basket chair. Perhaps the owner had just such a chair in his own house.

Since the human being within the urn has, through cremation, become formless, something definite must be done to help him retain his identity during the period that he is undergoing transformation. For a warrior, a helmet instead of a cup or overturned saucer is one answer. And so we have the helmet-urn as insurance against loss of personal identity. Helmeted in this world, the warrior will continue to be helmeted in the next. The gifts laid beside his urn will help: his sword, his spear, the bit he so often inserted in his horse's mouth, all these will help to identify him in the After World.

To make doubly sure that a person would retain his own appearance and identity, his features were often painted on his burial-urn, or a mask was made, representing him, and attached to the urn. One such mask, made of bronze and neatly fitted to a terracotta urn of the seventh century B.C., is in the museum at Chiusi. Its approximate height, including its helmet covering, is twelve and five-eighth inches. The slightly crooked nose and open mouth create a bizarre expression that is somehow rather attractive.

Etruscan helmets varied from the tall crested type to the plain, hemispherical helmet of bronze, now in the British Museum, which Hiero, the tyrant of Syracuse, sent to Olympia as a thank offering for his victory off Cumae in 474 B.C. The Greek inscription on the helmet states that it was part of the booty taken from the defeated Etruscan fleet.

The general similarity in helmet shapes and particularly in decorative designs has led some scholars to suggest that perhaps, even in Villanovan days, workmen may have traveled about the countryside fashioning various objects, such as helmets and shields, or household utensils, in more or less the same style.

Toward the beginning of the last century the Italian archaeologist, Boni, who excavated the large cemetery in the Roman Forum, discovered there a great many burial-urns shaped like those small round huts so often seen today in Italy where sheep and goats are grazing. Because of their shape, these burial-urns have come to be known as hut-urns. Similar hut-urns have been found in many places in Etruria, especially in the vicinity of Chiusi and Vetulonia; and they have also appeared in northern Germany.

Almost every museum has hut-urns on display. A terra-cotta hut-urn from Vetulonia now in the Archaeological Museum in Florence is perhaps the most typical and certainly one of the best preserved. Its walls, rounded as one would expect, since the round house is one of the early forms in many parts of the world, rest upon a projecting base; its eaves rise gently to a peak in the center and overhang the walls on all sides.

The squared doorway of this hut-urn is outlined by half a dozen or so deeply incised lines. A squared slab of terra-cotta that fits precisely into the doorway is decorated along its edges by zigzag lines that form the two equal legs of an isosceles triangle, each angle so formed pointing inward toward an incised square in the center. With a dislike of unused space almost equal to that of the Greek artist, the Etruscan artist has drawn in the center of his square slab, or door, as we should say, a fan of intersecting lines that run from corner to corner.

Rectangular hut-urns have also been found. On the first of the two upper floors of the Archaeological Museum in Florence there is a rectangular urn of alabaster, said to have belonged to the Buonarroti family. The portrayal on its lid of two warriors lifting a dead companion could well have inspired Michelangelo's *Pietà*. On the end wall, to your right, as you enter the room, a shelf supports another small rectangular urn shaped like a house, though for this urn mansion might be a better word.

This elegant little mansion has an arched entrance-door, with Ionic pilasters carved on either side. Similar arched doorways occur in Tuscan palaces of the Renaissance period. Looking at this beautifully modeled urn, you can not but feel yourself transported to the great days of Etruscan life when a privileged family dwelt in just such a mansion, served by silent-footed slaves and entertained with song and dance.

The use of hut-urns to receive the ashes of a deceased person springs from the same general and almost pervasive belief that he must continue to dwell in a receptacle as much like a house as possible. The small utensils that have been found with many of

41

these urns and in even larger quantities in many tombs are thought by some to indicate that Villanovans and Etruscans, like many other early peoples, believed the animating spirit, or soul, to be a dwarf-like figure that could dwell in a small space and that could make use of small utensils. Others believe that these small objects were only a child's playthings, left there because he would need them in the After World.

The Berlin Museum has an interesting example of these rectangular urns, one that I have seen only in photographs. Nearly seven feet high, including its stone platform, apparently an unusual feature, and what looks like a modern penthouse on its roof, this urn represents a departure from the ordinary type.

The platform under the urn is double; it creates the impression that one is looking at the model of a house perched on a wind-swept cliff, with a penthouse added for the view. The heavy sloping roof between the urn proper and the penthouse above adds to the impression that the cliff-house has been built to withstand the wind.

The entrance to this tall house-urn is through a broad rectangular doorway. The door is the usual stone slab with heavy door-jambs. Here instead of incised lines, which would be too slight for decorative purposes, the monument-builder has cut deep horizontal grooves along the upper edges of the double platform, and on the roof broad vertical lines. Altogether, this is a pleasant burial-urn in which to sleep while awaiting transformation and release and also one from which its occupant, if properly supplied with food and "blood-juice," would have no incentive to leave merely to vent his hostility upon any of the living who had neglected him.

Other variations in the form of burial-urns occur. The Louvre has a small terra-cotta urn of the sixth century B.C. that shows a dead man comfortably resting on his funeral couch, his body outstretched on a thick mattress and his head supported on a clumsy pillow. Both mattress and pillow are no doubt copies in terra-cotta of what the deceased had enjoyed in his own house.

The dead man is represented as fully clothed, his cap on his head, and on his feet the pointed shoes with curled-over tips, somewhat like the present-day Greek or Turkish peasant shoes but without the pompon, that were popular in sixth-century Etruria. Mayani has identified this dead man as Pumpus (Pompey) Scunas, a freedman. Part of his inscription reads that "with the fathers (he enjoys) a lasting sleep."

In the National Museum of Perugia, there is an urn from the famous Tomb of the Volumni family, which belongs to the second century B.C. after Perugia had become Romanized. The inscription notes that the occupant is a certain Arnth Velimnes Aules, a handsome man who, to judge from the great ring with a stone that covers almost four fingers of his right hand, may have been an official. In his left hand he holds an irregularly-shaped vessel of some kind. He, too, is fully clothed, but in a robe that is arranged in soft, easy folds over his body. His feet are not visible.

Half-reclining on his elaborately decorated funeral couch, his left arm and shoulder supported on two cushions, Arnth Velimnes is obviously a man of substance who has learned to accept things as they are. The funeral couch with its large square base forms a monument worthy of the dignified official on the lid.

The square base, or the lower part of the monument, in which the ashes of the deceased rest, is guarded by two winged male figures, partly facing each other across what appears to be a door, perhaps a gateway to the After World.

The belief underlying burial seems to have been that the urn is a sort of "hermetic vessel" in which the dead are to be transformed into powerful new beings. While this transformation is under way, the dead lie helpless in the urn, dependent upon the care of those they have left behind.

Upon the manner in which the survivors treat the deceased persons, in either a sarcophagus or an urn, depends the future attitude of the dead toward the living; whether one gains their help as powerful divinities, or their hostility as evil spirits who will bring harm. Those who were sleeping in their tombs, whether whole or in ash, needed blood. Cremation did not destroy that need.

To deprive the dead of blood was a crime that had to be expiated. This was the crime of the Etruscans who, in the sixth century B.C., stoned to death the crews of the ships they captured when their Phocaean enemies had to abandon Corsica and risk the danger of the sea between their island and the Italian coast.

The stoning occurred near Cerveteri. Herodotus tells us that the dead of Cerveteri showed their anger at being unnecessarily deprived of their portion of blood by sending upon their fellow-citizens an epidemic of sprains, broken bones, paralysis, and other crippling ills similar to those that stoning had inflicted upon the unfortunate crews. A general cutting of Phocaean throats would have been wiser, and more satisfactory to all concerned.

Unable to cope with what their own dead had sent upon them, the citizens of Cerveteri dispatched messengers to Greece, to the distant shrine of Delphi near Mount Parnassus, to beg advice. The oracle bade Cerveteri institute funeral games, consecrated to the memory of their dead. The funeral games were to consist of horse-racing and other competitive sports. When this had been done, the epidemic disappeared. Herodotus also reports that a hundred years later these games were still being held near Cerveteri.

Human sacrifice, though not specifically mentioned as a reason for funeral games, was undoubtedly implied, for in ancient days competitive games generally resulted in the death of one or more of the competitors. According to tradition, the Etruscans introduced to Campania in southern Italy the custom of holding gladiatorial combats in connection with funerals; the number and the nature of the combats probably came to be a status symbol. The dead gladiators were dragged out of the arena by a man disguised to resemble the snaky-headed Tuchuchla, the Etruscan demon of death. Later on, the Romans used a hook.

The sacrifice of human beings to fulfill the needs of the dead is thought to have persisted longer in Etruria than in Greece, where animals were early substituted. In Greek legend the goddess Artemis saved Iphigenia from death on the sacrificial altar by arriving at the last moment with a ram in her arms. The Book of the Mummy refers to blood-sacrifice as "dispensing life."

In the ancient city of Teotihuacán, which the Mexican archaeologist, Jorge Acosta, has recently excavated, blood was offered to a god of flowers. Teotihuacán, the site of the famous Pyramid of the Sun, once larger than either ancient Athens or Rome (*TIME* magazine, June 21, 1963) lies thirty-four miles northeast of Mexico City. Centuries after even the name of the city had been forgotten, the Aztecs came upon the half-buried site and called it Teotihuacán, the "place where men become gods." The blood-offering made to a deity of flowers in this vanished city of the fourth century B.C. came from the worshiper's finger or eyelids; he slashed them, let the blood "soak into porous paper," then burned the paper in a small clay bowl.

The Romans, in the third century B.C., influenced either by the Etruscan custom of sacrificing human beings or because they had succumbed to their own terror of a second imminent invasion of Gallic tribes from the North, buried alive in their cattle market two Gauls, a man and a woman as prophylactic sacrifices.

To ward off danger to one's country the blood of a member of one's own race was more efficacious, though, than that of an alien, especially if the blood were freely offered. That the Etruscans believed this to be true finds some proof in an engraving which Mayani reproduces from a study made in 1890 of the reliefs on Etruscan urns. The engraving shows two young men, (patricians, since they are fully clothed) one kneeling, the other standing.

Mayani describes the scene: "The face of the first displays an impressive serenity. Behind them are to be seen two sacrificants with upraised daggers, ready to immolate them. On the right of the group is a flute-player; on the left are two men-servants carrying tools and a ladder; the servant on the extreme left, in his emotion, has grasped his comrade's arm. According to Körte, the ladder is required for the ritual incineration which will follow."

The young patricians have offered their life's blood to save their country from danger. "The blood of prisoners is inadequate,"

Mayani explains, "in this supreme sacrifice; and Etruscan nobles are consequently prepared to give up their own." A dark page of Etruscan history? Not necessarily; love of country and patriotic fervor are dawning in this Golden Age of ancient Italy when the Etruscans believed, with Hesiod, of whom they may never have heard, that the sterner virtues of life were to be cultivated.

The trend of Etruscan thought may now be dimly glimpsed. From the seventh century B.C. on, Etruscan man is slowly becoming aware of himself and of his place in a world that is larger than himself, or even than his own aspirations. In this feeling, Etruscan man was not alone; the whole Mediterranean world was awakening to a fuller consciousness of the meaning of life and of death, and this new awareness was expressing itself in new burial modes. He was changing in other ways, too, but he was especially worried about the preservation of himself in the minds of others. Simplicity was retreating as the Etruscan world expanded. With this expansion came a new conception of life in the present and of life in the future.

The great mounds, the vaulted tomb structures, and the elaborately decorated burial-urns all proclaimed to the Mediterranean world and proclaims to the modern world as well, the new consciousness of Etruscan man. For the doctrine of Tages, as we shall see, had taught that, although man's days on earth were numbered, his life in the After World would be without end.

But the mighty god Tinia, who declared his will in roarings of thunder and flashes of lightning, feared lest Etruscan man, in his new consciousness, might lift his head too high above his feet. A stumble would bring him low, and his Golden Age would vanish. And so to help him keep his feet in the old ways, the great god Tinia resolved to send to the Etruscans in their adopted home his earth-born son, Tages.

PART TWO
THE SILVER AGE

". . . of silver and less noble by far. . . . for they
could not keep. . . . from wronging one another. . . ."

HESIOD, *Works and Days*

VI

Tages, the Earth-born

So shrouded in the mists of antiquity is the mysterious figure the Etruscans called Tages that neither history nor legend have succeeded in bringing him out into the clear light of day.

History knows Tages as the reputed author of what the centuries have passed down to us under various names: the *Tagetic Doctrine,* the *Libri Tagetici,* and the *Disciplina Etrusca.* The little that has survived from the original twelve books of this Doctrine comes to us at second hand from the fragments of two Latin translations: one by a noted Roman jurist, Marcus Labeo; the other by a certain Tarquinius Priscus. Both writers lived in the time of Augustus when ancient Etruria had become the seventh *regio,* or district, of the Roman Empire. To both Labeo and Priscus the Etruscan Tages was a law-giver. But the Doctrine comprised more than injunctions; it was a kind of Bible, to which no one had access except the *haruspices,* soothsayers, or high priests, who were trained to interpret the will of the gods by examining the internal organs of animals slain for sacrifice.

At the zenith of Tarquinia's glory there were in the city sixty of these religious officials, whose word was the law of the land. The *haruspices*—the name really means liver-scrutinizers—were also trained to read and interpret the will of the gods by observing the flight of birds and the direction from which flashes of lightning and crashes of thunder came.

Legend tells us more about Tages than history does, for legend can take us to the days when tales were the stuff out of which history grew.

"These were bright and sunny days in old Etruria," wrote Mrs. Hamilton Gray, after she returned from her visit to Etruria in 1839, "when every man sat under his own vine, and under his own fig-tree, when Tages taught him how to read fortunes from the swoop of an eagle's wing."

In those bright and sunny days legend whispered that Tages was a *Genius,* either the son or grandson of Tinia, the powerful god who, when the Etruscans had developed the concept of a divine hierarchy, stood at its head.

Legend also whispered into the ears of these early people that Tages had not come into the world in the usual fashion of the children of men. Tales of supernatural birth persist in all parts of the world, and ancient Etruria was no exception. One day a certain Tarchon, a Lydian and either the son or the brother of Tyrrhenus, but now a *lucumo* from Tarquinia, was plowing in his field near the city. Legend says that Tarchon had been assigned the Herculean task of building in the new land twelve cities. Among the twelve was the city known today as Tarquinia, though, according to epigraphical evidence from the tomb of the Tarquins, its original name was Tarchna.

As Tarchon plowed steadily on, turning up furrow after furrow of rich, virgin soil, suddenly there appeared before his astonished eyes a human head, partly risen from the furrow. The face was that of a young child, but the head was covered with gray hair.

Terrified by the apparition, Tarchon shouted for help. The other *lucumones,* who seem to have been conveniently near, no doubt plowing their own fields, for these were simple days, hastened to respond to Tarchon's appeal.

The apparition then revealed itself as Tages, sent by the great god

Tinia to impart to the *lucumones* the regulations by which they must teach their people to live. These laws the *lucumones* are said to have inscribed on waxen tablets. When the earth-sprung child had completed his mission, he sank back into the furrow and was seen no more. But not long ago the oldsters of the Tuscan countryside declared that, when their children were ill, Tago, their *spirito bambino,* would rise from the earth to help them, if properly invoked. This they told to Charles Leland, early in the last century when he was collecting the almost forgotten lore of the countryside for his book, *Etruscan Roman Remains in Popular Tradition.*

Leland has included in his book a fascinating illustration which, unfortunately, he does not explain. The illustration shows a tightly-swaddled infant, its face clearly visible. But on the lower part of the swaddled bundle appears the wrinkled face of an elderly man. Are we looking at Tages or at Tago? Leland does not say whether the illustration is a modern artist's conception of Tages-Tago, or a drawing of Tuscan ceramic that Leland discovered somewhere.

Tales of young children who speak words of wisdom or who are credited with healing powers are common to all folk lore, as Leland points out. He also points out that, since the earliest such legend in Europe is that of the "Etruscan infant known as Tages," the resemblance between the two legends is worthy of note. Tages was born with gray hair. But in Lydia, Tarchon was also said to have been born with a hoary head. The attribution of gray hair to each actor in this goblin-like legend has caused some scholars to feel that Tages and Tarchon were originally the same individual. In ancient times, however, they seem to have been separate individuals. Today, Tages has apparently survived in Tuscan folk lore, and Tarchon has not.

In Etruscan art Tages appears both as a child and as an adolescent boy. Two small bronzes now in the Gregorian Museum of the Vatican have been provisionally identified as the child Tages. One was found in Perugia, the other in Tarquinia, and both were sent to Rome. The statuette from Tarquinia has an Etruscan inscription on its right arm. When I went to the Vatican to see the statues, I had expected to find them in the room of the bronzes and the jewelry in the Gregorian Museum, one near the head of the bronze bed from Larthia's tomb, the other near a window. Neither statue was in the indicated place. Nor had any one ever heard of the child Tages. Finally an attendant took me to a room where a beautiful bronze statue stood.

"Ecco," he said, triumphantly. "That is what you want."

The statue was the exquisite Mars from Todi.

I thanked my attendant, admired the Mars, and continued my search. In a nearby room I found the statues. Each portrays a small boy seated cross-legged on the ground. The artist has included in both portraits the traditional *bulla* which every Roman child of patrician birth, boy or girl, wore suspended from his neck until he reached maturity, an Etruscan custom Tarquin the Elder is said to have brought with him when he came to Rome.

The *bulla* was a small bubble-shaped locket, often of gold, that contained an amulet or a charm against both sickness and the dreaded Evil Eye. In Etruria, when the child arrived at maturity, he dedicated his *bulla* to his domestic gods. Perhaps the Roman child did, too.

After the Second Punic War the privilege of wearing the *bulla* was extended to all children of free birth. The only adults who were permitted to wear the *bulla* were Roman generals, and then only when they were celebrating a triumph. The reason for this permission being given is easily understood. A triumphant general must be protected from the jealous wrath of the gods.

Some one has suggested that the antidote, or charm against evil, contained in the *bulla* may have been a sprig of asafoetida, a resinous gum that smells like garlic. This is a reasonable suggestion, since it is well known that among early peoples strong smells are efficacious in warding off evil. Modern man says that he "catches" a cold or a disease. Ancient man knew that the evil thing "caught" him, and that he had to be constantly on his guard. Amulets afforded the needed protection.

The bronze statuette from Tarquinia with the Etruscan inscription on its right arm is included among the three representations of the mythical Tages in the *Museum Etruscum* by Antonio Francesco Gori. This three-volume work, published toward the middle of the eighteenth century, contains three hundred copper plate engravings that illustrate all phases of Etruscan life. One page of the second volume is devoted to Tages.

The bronze statuette is the only seated figure represented. The other two are standing figures, one of an adolescent boy, the other of a child.

The child holds with both hands what seem to be the handles of an invisible plow; the adolescent boy's right hand holds an object somewhat difficult to describe. Both figures are fully clothed, the child in a straight robe that reaches to his feet, which are shod in slippers with upturned toes, and the boy in a robe of Roman cut that reaches halfway to his bare feet, but leaves his right shoulder and torso exposed. The object he holds in his right hand could be either a long-stemmed flower or a serpent with protruding tongue.

The page on which these three representations appear is labeled TAGES. The child with the plow is not specifically named. The adolescent boy stands on a low base with the words GENIUS TAGETIS inscribed on it; he is the *Genius* of Tages.

The seated statuette from Tarquinia and the adolescent boy in the Roman-style garment wear the Etruscan *bulla;* the child with the plow does not. This might mean that the child, if he is our earth-sprung Tages of divine parentage, does not need to be protected against evil. The adolescent boy may be merely a votive offering, as some think, and not the youthful *haruspex* on the Tarchon mirror, with his feet ritually bare, but the child surely is meant to represent the mysterious being who sprang from the plowed furrow near Tarquinia and dictated to the Etruscans the way of life they were to follow.

Von Vacano thinks that three bronze intaglios found during the excavation of some tombs near Tarquinia may also refer to the Tages legend. On each intaglio a human head is shown rising from the earth into the midst of a group of people who appear to hold writing tablets in their hands.

Representations of Tages occur frequently on Etruscan mirrors. The engraving on the back of the so-called Tarchon mirror is one of the best known, and one of the most controversial. This handsome bronze mirror—about five inches wide and generally considered a work of the third century B.C.—is now in the Archaeological Museum in Florence. It was found toward the end of the nineteenth century in Toscanella, not far from Tarquinia. Both the back of the mirror and the handle are engraved, the back with a group of five persons, the handle with what seems to be Atlas, who in Greek mythology supports the world on his shoulders. Here he supports the world on his upturned hands.

In the center of the group of five persons pictured on the back of the mirror stands a youthful figure, his left foot resting on a rock. He holds in his right hand a large liver with pendent lobes. Near by stands a bearded man who closely watches the young man's fingers as they touch the upper surface of the liver. The other members of the group also watch.

The young man and his older companion are both clothed in garments such as one occasionally sees illustrated in Etruscan art: a cone-shaped hat, a short-sleeved undergarment, and a pleated cloak that falls just below the knees. This was the distinctive garb of the liver-scrutinizer, or *haruspex*. In this costume, and with bare feet, contrary to the usual Etruscan custom of going shod, a *haruspex* would always be recognized and respected.

Above the head of each *haruspex* represented on this hand mirror a name is written in Etruscan characters: *Tarchunos* over the head of the older man, *pavetarchies* over the head of the younger man. The second half of the latter word, *tarchies,* von Vacano thinks may be *Tarchet,* the Etruscan for Tages.

The scene has been variously interpreted. Pallotino, the well known Etruscologist of the University of Rome, thinks it may be a lesson in the art of divination from an examination of the liver of a sacrificial animal. Some who follow von Vacano in his identification of the youthful figure as Tages feel that he may be instructing Tarchon, who plowed him up out of his field. To this von Vacano himself objects, since legend represents Tages as a hoary-headed child, not as a youthful teacher.

Von Vacano and Ducati interpret the scene as representing a ritual that may have been performed at the founding of Tarquinia, in which a *haruspex* would have played the principal rôle. The other members of the group would then be "interested observers, perhaps spirits or minor deities."

The belief in *Genii,* that is, spirits or minor deities, von Vacano thinks, is what gives its "special peculiarity" to Etruscan mythology. But under different names and in different guises *Genii* appear in other mythologies as well. The legend of Aladdin's lamp will occur to every one.

Mayani offers an entirely different interpretation of the scene on the Tarchon mirror. The bearded man, *Tarchunos,* is not Tarchon, the frightened plowman, but Tarquin the Elder, the first Etruscan king of Rome. The woman who stands beside him is Ucerseia, or Ocresia, about whom several versions of a strange story are told. Mayani recounts two versions, but since the full story is connected with the birth of Mastarna, or Servius Tullius, I shall keep it for a later chapter.

The words *pava Tarchies* (hyphenated by von Vacano) that are written over the young man's head mean, according to Mayani, "Tarchies saw," *pava* being the past tense of an Illyrian word, "and therefore Etruscan and Albanian." The young man, a soothsayer and expert in divination as set forth in the so-called Tagetic Doctrine, has been summoned to the palace in Rome to interpret what the woman Ocresia said she saw in Tarquin's hearth-fire, beside which she had been ordered to sit.

The leading part in the scene on the mirror belongs then, according to Mayani, to Ocresia, who in one version of the story is a slave, in another the captured daughter of a king whose city Tarquin has destroyed.

The most characteristic feature of the Tages legend is, we recall, that he was born with a hoary head. An attempt to portray this feature seems to have been made on two mirrors, one in the British Museum, and the other in the Royal Museum of Berlin. The mirror in the British Museum is called the "Toilet of Helen." On its handle, drawn in fine incised lines, is a portrait of a small nude boy with a *bald* head that some think was intended to represent the hoary-headed Tages.

The Berlin mirror shows a nude boy with a partly bald head who has also been identified as Tages. But here we have something more. The birth-story has been changed. Tages is the offspring of the Etruscan counterparts of the Roman Hercules and Minerva. This variation in the legend we learn from the names inscribed in Etruscan characters above the heads of each of the four adults who are grouped around the nude child.

The child, who is seated in the palm of his father's hand, is the only member of the group without a name inscribed above him. Obviously, his partly bald head is enough identification.

The names written above three of the adults are Turan, who is the Etruscan counterpart of Aphrodite, the Greek goddess of love, Menrva, or Minerva, the goddess of wisdom, and Hercle, or Hercules. The fourth name, Munthuch, is still a mystery. Turan seems to be only a bystander, but the engraver has probably introduced her to indicate the relationship between Hercules and Minerva, the parents of the nameless child. As if to assert her maternal rights or to keep the child from tumbling out of his father's hand, Minerva holds him firmly by one arm. But the child disregards his mother and turning to his father reaches out toward him.

Gerhard, who includes this engraving in his study of Etruscan mirrors, accepts the legend that regards the child as Tages and the offspring of Hercules and Minerva, each a deity in his own right. It is interesting to reflect that even if a variant legend has forgotten or has discarded the relationship between Tages and the great god Tinia, he still remains of divine or semi-divine birth. Perhaps Tages is in the process of becoming Tago.

Pliny the Elder, who died during the eruption of Vesuvius in

79 A.D., has left us in the second book of his *Natural History* a brief account of the Etruscan belief in the sacred hierarchy of the gods. Tinia, as the head of the hierarchy, sat enthroned on a summit in the north. At his feet lay the south. With a sweep of his eye, he created east and west, and these became the quarters in which the sun rises and sets on a lateral axis that bisects the heavens.

To the left of the god, where the constellations rise, lay that part of heaven's vault which the gods called propitious; to his right lay the unpropitious part.

Von Vacano explains this seeming contradiction: to a suppliant who stands facing Tinia, the reverse would be true; to him the right would be propitious, the left unpropitious.

Dividing the heavens into four quarters did not, however, provide adequate housing for Tinia's large family of divine beings. And so he subdivided the four quarters into eight, and again into sixteen. According to Pliny, then, the divine world which Tinia ruled consisted of sixteen gods.

Of the sixteen only twelve were great gods, and of the twelve only eight had the right to hurl thunderbolts. Each of the eight had his own special bolt, which could be recognized by its distinctive color. To the *haruspex* each bolt was recognizable, since he knew the fixed position in the heavens from which each god hurled his bolt.

But the eight were subject to the twelve, and the twelve were subject to a nameless, dread power of which even a *haruspex* stood in awe. To see one man struck down, while another beside him stood unhurt, was surely evidence of an awful power, unpredictable in its actions, incomprehensible in its results.

Even Tinia was subject to the nameless power, though to a lesser degree than were the others. For Tinia had the privilege of wielding "three glittering red thunderbolts." The first he could hurl at his own discretion. The second, which could bring about both good and evil at the same time, he could hurl only if all twelve gods had previously given their consent. The third and last bolt was the most fearful and the most destructive of all. Permission to hurl this final bolt had to be secured from the power shrouded in darkness that even the gods might not penetrate.

Pliny's description tallies remarkably well with a bronze model of a sheep's liver discovered in the nineteenth century in Piacenza, an Italian town north of the Apennines. The model, roughly circular, has sixteen compartments in its outer ring, where the powerful deities live, each presumably with his name-plate affixed. Several inner circles are also divided into compartments for the lesser gods.

According to Pallotino, the Tagetic Doctrine envisioned a universe in which the "great superior deities, strongly individualized and generally favorable, were placed in the eastern sectors of the sky, especially in the north-eastern; the gods of the earth and of nature were towards the south; the infernal deities and the gods of fate, inexorable and fearful, were supposed to inhabit the dread regions of the west, especially the north-west, considered to be the most inauspicious of all."

Some historians seem to think that the original Etruscan conception of the universe was a simpler thing. To anthropologists, however, who feel that the mind of early man progressed from the complex to the simple, it seems far more likely that the Etruscans believed in a multiplicity of gods, rather than in a few, and that they slowly arrived, as did other peoples, at the idea of one supreme deity who built the universe.

The question that comes at once to mind is how an augur learned the will of these distant gods. Mayani explains the procedure that may have been used. The augur drew a square on the ground, then bisected and quartered the square. Each quarter was then subdivided, and as the bronze model shows, placed under the protection of its deity, probably by tracing in the ground the name of the divine resident. Since the ground plan now mirrors, as it were, the divine plan, the augur, by placing himself where the lines intersect and observing over which section the omen appears, will know which deity is responsible.

Whether the original Tagetic Doctrine included some such link between heaven and earth, we do not know, but it seems certain that it contained the bulk of Etruscan religious erudition, and that the *haruspices* used the Doctrine to control the whole life of Etruscan man, from the day of his birth to the day of his death. He was taught to believe that all the sciences—considered secular today—were an essential part of religion, and that he could not interpret them for himself. Deprived of freedom to think, he believed implicitly in revelation and in a doctrine that "affirmed the possibility of direct communication with supernatural forces."

For tangible proof of revelation and of the "possibility of direct communication," the Etruscan had his belief in the earth-sprung Tages, the scion of great Tinia, who had bridged the chasm between god and man. Under the guidance of Tages, and that of his representative, the *haruspex,* Etruscan man might, when his time came, also bridge the chasm and become a god.

By the time of the Roman Emperors Tages had acquired a reputation almost equal to that of the Delphic oracle. But Tages had a rival, an Etruscan woman, Vegoia, or Begoe, whose books on divination were long preserved in the temple of Apollo at Rome. The respect accorded Vegoia was typical of the general Etruscan attitude toward women. This attitude was rooted in the distant past when each family had its own sacred fire, its own hearth, and its own domestic gods. To that distant past may belong Mrs. Gray's idyllic picture of sunny days in old Etruria when "every man sat under his own vine, and under his own fig-tree."

VII

The Family and Its Housing

Primitive Indo-European civilization regarded the family as a sacred society, almost a church. According to the Laws of Manu, this was also true of the Hindus. The Code, or Laws of Manu, discusses the Hindu conception of the creation of the world, the state of the soul after death, and the purpose of the family. A closed society, the family existed solely for the procreation of children, especially sons. Daughters were needed, only as they could provide the nourishing ground for the seed of a man from another closed society.

When a daughter left the society she had been born into, she severed all further connection with it; its sacred fire could no longer cook her meals nor feed her lonely spirit; she belonged to another household, to her husband, not to her father. If she proved sterile or produced only daughters, she was returned to her father, for in this early stratum of Indo-European life, sterility was more often blamed upon the female than upon the male.

Sons could procreate other sons and so keep the family intact. An intact family included all its members, living or dead, and the dead members could survive only if the living members brought to them in their places of burial the food and drink they needed to sustain them while they awaited their release into the next world.

If a man was so unfortunate as to die without leaving behind him male offspring, his widow would be married to a brother or other relative of her husband's. Children, born of this second union, whether sons or daughters, were counted as belonging to the woman's first husband.

These customs, inherited from the earliest stratum of Indo-European civilization, were common to the Greeks, the Romans, the Hindus, and were probably also common to the Etruscans, since their effects can be traced in later laws. Though the Etruscans seem to have broken away from many other inherited customs before the Greeks or the Romans or the Hindus, they were still bound by the strongest of all possible chains, the necessity of keeping the family intact.

Each family, or sacred society, had its own private burial-field where its departed members lived on under the ground, just as the family they were temporarily separated from lived in its own individual housing. This arrangement, according to de Coulanges, lies at the root of man's age-old need of private ownership. Religion, not law, first "guaranteed the right of property." This was true of the Greeks, the Romans, the Etruscans, and the Hebrews, since all these peoples were united in the same fundamental religious belief.

A fragment, ascribed to Vegoia and preserved in Latin, makes it clear that her people held firmly to the god-given right of every family to its "portion of soil." But the god who gave this right was not the creator who is mentioned in the Etruscan cosmogony.

"The gods who conferred upon every family its right to a portion of the soil, were the domestic gods, the sacred fire, and the manes." The *manes,* a word constantly used in books on Roman religion, were, to adopt the modern terminology, the spirits of the dead.

Diodorus Siculus, a Greek historian who lived in the time of Augustus, says that the sacred fire taught men to "build houses." And so men became differentiated from the birds of the air and the beasts of the field.

Upon that portion of land a man considered his own he built

his house, to shelter his sacred fire, his hearth which no one outside his family might approach, since under the stone lived his gods. For this reason the fire must never be quenched, except upon the one prescribed day of the year, when the fire was ceremonially put out, and as ceremonially relighted. Quenching this fire in any other manner would cause the death of the whole family, which included its ancestors.

"Thus the hearth-fire is a sort of moral being," writes de Coulanges, "it shines, and warms, and cooks the sacred food; but at the same time it thinks, and has a conscience. . . . One might call it human. . . . it blazes up, it moves, it lives. . . . it has sentiments and affections, it gives man purity. . . ."

The man's first house may have been a round hut, built of wattle and with a thatched roof. Round huts such as these are believed by archaeologists to have been the first dwellings built in the place that afterwards became the Roman Forum. Wood soon gave way to stone, since the house was intended for generation after generation of the same family. Though we have no evidence that Etruscan houses were ever built of stone, since nothing has survived except the tombs, it seems probable that their buildings followed the same general pattern found in the rest of the Mediterranean world.

Unfortunately, our only real guide to the structure of the Etruscan house is the structure of the Etruscan tomb, supplemented by what we can learn from its wall-paintings, from scenes depicted on burial-urns and sarcophagi, and for later houses, from reconstructed dwellings of ancient Pompeii.

The many-chambered Etruscan tomb must have been as exact a reproduction of an Etruscan mansion as family ingenuity and wealth could manage, for it, like a dwelling on the surface of the earth, was intended for the immediate family and for future generations. Just as the sacred fire was ceremonially quenched upon the prescribed days of the year, so upon prescribed days of the year (probably also stated in the Tagetic Doctrine) the entire family brought food and drink to the ancestral tomb to share with the dead.

This ancient custom is still preserved in Yugoslavia, where during Pentecost the Vlachs celebrate the Pomana, or festival of the dead. Carrying food and drink on their way to the cemeteries, the Vlachs sing dirges to their dead, inviting them to come forth and join in the feast. The Vlachs also bring water, and invite the dead to wash themselves. In Etruria, too, the dead had to be invited. The festival closes with dancing in which all join.

Etruscan family meals, or feasts, which they also held in honor of the dead, often appear in the tomb paintings. So realistic are these portrayals that you feel they must certainly have been modeled upon scenes drawn from daily life.

Until recently, visitors to a little known tomb not far from Tarquinia could have seen painted on its wall two charming family scenes. In the first painting they would have seen, prominent in the foreground, a low table with three vases, or jars.

The jar in the center would have been recognized as a *krater*, or bowl for mixing wine with water, as was the custom in other parts of the Mediterranean world. Flanking the *krater* on either side, stood two black-figured burial-jars, decorated in late seventh-century style, black figures on a reddish background. From these three vases the tomb acquired its name: the Tomb of the Painted Vases. Penetrating deeper into the tomb, the visitors would have seen that its ceiling was white, with small red flowers sprinkled liberally over its surface, a copy perhaps of the ceiling in some pleasant Tarquinian home.

These charming family scenes were on the side walls of the tomb, each painting in such sad condition now, faded and defaced, that the tomb is closed to the public. Fortunately, early travelers to Etruria were privileged to enter; and one of them, Mary A. Johnstone, has left us a vivid description, which I have taken the liberty of curtailing and reproducing here.

Each scene portrays an Etruscan family, parents and small children, dining *al fresco* in the garden. The smiling parents recline on their dining-couch, the children sit at their feet: in one scene a brother and a sister, in the other two little sisters. The table, set with food, is drawn within easy reach of the couch. No table implements are visible.

The first scene includes the family pet, a dog or leopard, who crouches under the table, patiently waiting for his share of the meal. The brother and sister wait, too, though not so patiently, for the boy's left arm is around his sister's shoulder, as if to restrain her, or to direct her attention to the fluttering dove he holds in his right hand. The boy is nude, like the young slave who waits near by, ready to serve his masters. The little girl is simply dressed in a loose garment that falls to her feet.

In the other scene, the two little girls, both fully dressed, hold garlands of flowers, as they sit quietly beside each other on the end of their parents' dining-couch. Their mother also holds a garland; she is presenting it to her husband. A special occasion this is, and we are privileged to attend, to admire the jewels worn by both husband and wife, as they sit listening to the music a slave-girl plays. Only one slave-boy attended the other family; here two stand waiting the master's call.

Unknown families, both of them, for no inscription seems to have accompanied either painting. The two black-figured vases tell us, though, that we are in the seventh century, when Etruscan life was still simple, when husband and wife dined together on the same couch, the custom so misunderstood by the Greeks and the Romans. Every one knows that a respectable Greek never allowed his wife to share his meals; his bed, yes, but not his meals.

After the fourth century B.C., judging from the changes to be seen on the lids of many later sarcophagi, husband and wife no longer reclined together at their meals. The husband reclines, the wife sits at his feet. Perhaps the children have been banished to the nursery, as often happens when society becomes affluent. Soon, in deference, must we say, to Roman custom, the Etruscan wife will sit on a chair or a stool, completely Romanized.

The two scenes just described are believed to portray seventh-century family life, but so easy is it to cross the thin line between life and death that we may also be looking at what the Etruscans believed would happen in the After World. Let us look at a scene from a family tomb near Orvieto.

Two elderly brothers are seated side by side on a couch. An inscription written over their heads introduces them; they are Velio and Arnth, sons of Larth, of the family Velii. The inscription adds that both brothers held religious offices.

With the two elderly men sits a seven-year-old boy; he is not nude, as the little boy in the first scene was, but clothed in white. Before the three motionless figures stands the funeral table, its candles lighted, its food ready to be served by the waiting slaves.

The little boy's name is Vel. If the scene is set in the After World, Vel is probably wearing the shroud he was buried in. Three members of the family Velii have already arrived; the table is spread to welcome the older son; he is on his way and soon they will see him, young and handsome, driving his chariot and horses home.

While the family waits, two musicians entertain them. You can see them standing near the foot of the table, one with his lyre, the other with the double pipes, both favorite instruments of the Etruscans.

The family Velii was doubtless well-to-do; for another scene in the same tomb shows us the kitchen. On the walls hang a side of beef, a deer, ducks, hares, and birds. Nude slaves bustle about, chopping meat, scrubbing tables, tending the great oven. The slaves have their music, too, and a monkey on a pole to add to their pleasure. Dining together in this fashion is one of the many proofs that in Etruscan life husband and wife were on terms of perfect equality, both in the present and in the After World that Tages had revealed to them.

Equality between husband and wife did not exist in that early stratum of Indo-European civilization which fathered the Greeks, the Romans, and the Hindus. Nor is it probable that equality existed among the Lydians, even that segment which is thought (by some) to have emigrated to Italy.

How far the Etruscans had advanced beyond the primitive attitude becomes clear from even a casual inquiry into Indo-European marriage rites.

"The first institution that the domestic religion established, probably," writes de Coulanges, "was marriage."

The first wrench for a young girl would be when she had to give up her domestic religion, the hearthstone of her father, the god whose sacred fire she had tended since childhood, for the "same person cannot invoke two sacred fires or two series of ancestors."

"From the hour of marriage," de Coulanges quotes one ancient source as saying, "the wife has no longer anything in common with the domestic religion of her fathers; she sacrifices at the hearth of her husband."

The first step toward marriage was taken at the paternal hearthstone. Here the girl's father sacrificed, and declared aloud that he was giving his daughter over into the keeping of another domestic hearth. Ritually severed from her former life, the young girl then accompanied her husband-to-be to his paternal hearth. Lustral (cleansing) water was sprinkled over her. She touched the sacred fire and repeated the prayers. Then the young couple broke bread together. They were now man and wife.

A *celebe,* a jar with pillared handles, in the Gregorian Museum is decorated with what is thought to be a wedding procession. Two young Etruscans are seated side by side in a four-horse chariot. The groom may be taking the bride to his own father's home, or the Etruscans may have advanced to the point where the young man will have a home of his own and be taking his bride there.

A wine-jug in the Archaeological Museum in Florence shows a young girl with her head veiled. With her is another young woman whose head is not veiled. The veiled girl is giving her hand to a young man who is, according to some interpreters, supposed to be the groom. Perhaps we are looking at part of the marriage ceremony in which the two in the four-horse chariot have just participated.

Marriage existed for the procreation of children. In Etruscan art children are represented so often that we feel Etruscan parents must have been fond of their children, and especially overjoyed at the birth of a son.

In a room of the Villa Giulia a seated woman, sculptured in stone, holds on her lap four mummy-like small creatures; she is the Roman goddess, *Mater Matuta,* some think, who takes all children under her care. The four small creatures huddled together on her lap might represent small deities, or perhaps a set of Etruscan quadruplets she is trying to save from being put to death as monstrosities.

We know so little of details such as these.

A terra-cotta group in another room of the Villa Giulia is composed of two figures, a man and a woman seated beside each other. A scarf covers both their heads. The man holds a *patera;* the woman an infant on her knee. Perhaps they are parents about to offer thanks, by pouring a libation, for the birth of a child.

The strong human mother clasping her child to her breast is frequently represented in Etruscan art. Sometimes the infant is nude; more often it is swaddled. Even without archaeological evidence, that infants were swaddled may be taken for granted. Italian mothers in country districts still swaddle their babies for the first three months of their lives, sometimes even longer. Urban mothers have discarded the practice, yet occasionally on the streets of Rome a mother may be seen with a swaddled baby in her arms, museum pieces, both of them.

Visitors to Florence will recall the frieze over the portico of the Hospital of the Innocents with della Robbia's swaddled *bambini* who smile down upon the passersby.

In 1839, Mrs. Hamilton Gray saw in a private collection of Etruscan antiquities a statuette of an infant in swaddling bands that had been found in a tomb beside the corpse of a warrior.

Since no funeral honors were permitted to infants, Mrs. Gray suggests that the Etruscan way of warding off pollution may have been similar to that of the Greeks. A person, presumed dead, over whom the final rites had been performed, could not, after recovery, enter a temple or sacred precinct until he had been washed and wrapped like a newborn infant, "emblematic of beginning life anew." Something of this sort may have happened to the warrior, and the swaddled image placed beside him to indicate that he had been reborn.

Revered though the Etruscan mother of a family may have been, the chances are that she had had no voice in choosing her husband, nor any control over her dowry. The prostitution that the Roman comic poet, Plautus, accused young Etruscan girls of indulging in to earn their dowries was possibly based upon a misunderstanding of a Lydian religious custom. Lydian girls, Herodotus notes, were required by the goddess Cybele, a goddess of fertility, to sacrifice their virginity to any male devotee who asked it of them.

Our impression of the high status enjoyed by the Etruscan woman (always a mark of advanced civilization) is confirmed by funeral inscriptions that frequently add the name of a man's mother to that of his father. In Spain a man maintains his mother's identity by combining her maiden name with his father's surname.

Though we are dependent for most of our understanding about the way these people lived on the structure of their tombs and burial-urns, and on the paintings and carvings shown there, we shall learn more if we visit a reconstructed mansion in Pompeii. The center of the mansion is the atrium, an Etruscan word adopted by the Romans. The atrium, or patio, is spacious, with a shallow pool of water in its center to catch the rain.

From the atrium we walk through room after room, their walls decorated with mythological scenes and dancing-girls, or brightly-plumaged birds, realistically painted. In the rear we shall find a garden, its trees and flowers kept fresh by a stream of water that has been piped in. Yes, this would have been the way a wealthy Etruscan or Roman family lived in Pompeii before Vesuvius put an end to it all. In the days of her greatness some of Tarquinia's mansions may have resembled just such a Pompeian house, though here we might have admired a fishing scene painted on a wall, with a man standing in the stern of his boat, waiting the favorable moment to cast his harpoon.

Tall candelabra add to the light that comes through the narrow windows. When weary of sightseeing, we may rest upon a couch, or seat ourselves in a bowl-shaped chair made for a canopic-urn. Or we may prefer a throne-like chair with a foot stool, or a folding-stool like one that the master of the house usually carries with him when he goes to view a spectacle.

We know nothing about the dwelling-places of the poor. As usual, the poor vanish, leaving little or no trace behind. Only a few relics from the pit-graves, pathetic gifts to mollify their ancestors who doubtless were poorer than they.

Though we know nothing about separate dwelling-places for the poor, it is safe to conclude that in the days when the Etruscan *lucumones* held full control over the land, those we would now class as the poor had enough to eat and drink, since their lives were probably spent in constant tendance upon their betters, who housed them, fed them, and buried them in return for their services. Rebellion against this mode of life came much later in the Etruscan world, when the acquisition of wealth brought about class distinctions in dress and in personal adornment that roused the "poor" to insist upon their rights. The first serious revolt occurred in Volsinia in the third century B.C.

VIII

Clothing and Toilet Accessories

The universal custom in the ancient world of swaddling an infant during his first months of life may have provided an early opportunity for distinguishing between a patrician child and his inferior. Embroidered bands of softer material and a *bulla* of gold around his neck would set the patrician child apart from the less fortunate infants of a great household. If a patrician mother knew that Aristotle advised binding infant limbs to keep them straight, she must have looked anxiously at her child's legs, whenever she unbound him, to make sure they were not crooked.

Though the air of the underground tombs of Etruria, unlike that of Egypt, was not conducive to preserving textiles, the minute fragments of materials that have recently been found make it probable that some swaddling bands could have been softer than others. If this can be assumed, an early distinction in infant clothing may then be assumed. Also, since an Etruscan gentleman sometimes wore a painted or embroidered mantle, perhaps the swaddling bands of a patrician child really were embroidered.

However, the true distinction between a patrician child and his inferior, especially in the days of Etruscan greatness, lay in the material of the *bulla*. The patrician child could wear a *bulla* of gold; his inferior, one of bronze, or even perhaps of wood.

Since in the Etruscan paintings a patrician boy is usually shown dressed, the small nude boy in the wall-painting (described by Mary Johnstone) who sits with his arm around his sister's shoulder must be an exception, for in general only male slaves and athletes appear unclothed. Small boys and girls of the *lucumo* set are almost always shown dressed alike, in plain, straight garments, fastened with brooches at the shoulder, or tied with a sash around the waist, and reaching well below the knees.

Early frescoes and bas-reliefs show men wearing a kind of embroidered kilt, which left the upper part of the body bare, a costume frequently seen in Minoan-Mycenaean frescoes. Later on, probably under Greek influence, Etruscan men wore a kind of *chiton,* or short tunic, similar to what was worn by the Greeks of the same period, except that Etruscan men seem to have had a stronger preference for bright colors.

In cold weather Etruscan men wore a heavy woolen cloak, called the *tebennos,* the forerunner of the Roman toga. When worn by a *haruspex,* the *tebennos* was fringed, but neither embroidered nor painted in gay colors. During the Empire, a high Roman official sometimes appeared, on state occasions, dressed in a toga on which portraits of members of his family had been painted. Usually, though, only the Emperor was privileged to wear such an elaborately decorated garment.

An interesting statuette, from Cerveteri but now in the British Museum and belonging, presumably, to the end of the seventh century B.C., shows a seated man who wears a round-necked close-fitting robe that reaches to his ankles. His left arm is covered to the wrist, his right to the elbow. The entire robe is criss-crossed with vertical and diagonal lines, almost as if the material had been tucked.

Women were modestly dressed in tunics, generally short-sleeved, made of light, pleated material, often embroidered, that also reached the ankles. In cold weather, the women, like the men, wore heavy cloaks.

Both men and women wore a sort of high toque, or *tutulus,*

pointed at the top and drawn well down over the ears, or at times rolled back and exposing the ears. This headgear the Etruscans may have brought with them from their Lydian home. When worn by a *haruspex,* the *tutulus* was fastened by bands knotted under the chin. The Louvre has many delightful little bronze figures of young women, or perhaps female divinities, each wearing the high, pointed toque.

Boys were either bare-headed or wore a sort of beret. In a wall-painting from the Tomb of Hunting and Fishing in Tarquinia, a boy with a beret on his head is diving from a high peak into the sea.

Fashions in headgear varied from region to region. In the upper Po valley men and women wore a broad-brimmed hat which, lower down in Tuscany, only slaves wore. Visitors to the Villa Giulia used to pause in astonishment before the Warrior from Capostrino, so strange was it to see a fighting-man wearing a broad-brimmed hat. The Warrior has now returned to the village he came from.

A sacrificial scene engraved on the back of a mirror shows a priest and a flute-player on either side of a blazing altar. Each is fully dressed, even to his cap. Two younger figures, one clinging to a balky goat, the other standing behind the priest, also wear caps, though both are as nude as the day they were born. Since the goat is obviously to be the victim, the god to be honored must be Fufluns, the Etruscan Bacchus. Perhaps some vineyard owner, disturbed by a poor grape harvest, has asked the priest to call upon Bacchus for help.

Changes in hair-styling have always varied from century to century. The story of the Spartans, combing out their long hair before the battle of Thermopylae, is familiar to every one. The Persian spies, looking down upon the Spartans from the secret path a Greek renegade had led them to, could not believe that fighting-men who were combing their hair could be ready for battle. If the Persian spies had waited, they might have seen the Spartans wrap their hair around their heads to cushion the shock of a blow on their metal helmets.

The Etruscan sarcophagi show men with their hair parted in the middle, braided, and reaching well down toward the middle of the body. In battle they also wore helmets. Perhaps they, too, wrapped these braids around their heads to cushion them against a blow. In the fifth century B.C. young men began to wear their hair short. The beards so often seen on early sarcophagi went out of fashion, especially for young men, when it became popular to imitate clean-shaven Greek youths.

Women's hair styles were as changeable in ancient Etruria as they are today. The sarcophagi show hair braided and falling over the shoulder, or drawn up and caught into a knot at the back of the neck. Later the braids are replaced by curls that frame the face and are very attractive. The fifth century saw the braids re-turn, but wrapped around the head under a tight cap. Since the Etruscans, so far as we know, were not a curly-haired people, their women must have had ways of curling their hair. Dennis had the good fortune to see a pair of curling-irons in a small museum in the Palazzo Baglioni, which at that time housed the discoveries made near Perugia in 1840.

No cosmetic box was found in Larthia's tomb, but bronze boxes with traces of pastes and ointments have been discovered in other tombs, along with the small spatulas for applying them. Perhaps these bronze boxes also contained dyes for changing the color of one's hair, because some of the frescoes represent women with blond hair. Natural or not, it may well have been that even thou-sands of years ago gentlemen preferred their ladies blond.

We have no evidence of beauty-parlors for the Etruscan ladies, but Etruscan gentlemen had special shops where they went to have excess hair removed from their bodies. These depilatory shops used pitch instead of razors. Though the Etruscans had depilatory shops, they had no barber shops, as the Greeks had, at least not before the middle of the fifth century B.C., when barbers came into Italy from Sicily.

Adult Etruscans, unlike adult Greeks and Romans, are seldom shown with bare feet. The two men on the Tarchon mirror whose feet are bare are religious officials. Doubtless the rule that still forbids either infidel or believer to enter an Oriental mosque, without removing his shoes, is of ancient origin.

Cobblers in Etruria were in great demand because of their fine craftsmanship, and because of the quality of the leather they used. Often the demand from Athens and from Rome exceeded the supply, and orders had to be sent far in advance. Shoes were made not only of leather, often with gilt thongs, but of various embroidered materials. High at the back and with pointed toes that curled over, Etruscan shoes resembled modern Oriental slippers.

A pair of sandals that were found at the site of the recently excavated city of Marzobotto near Bologna are more like clogs than sandals, and substantial enough to be used in the muddiest of Marzobotto's river swamps. The long broad-headed nails that were used must have required, as one authority speculates, "a sole an inch and a half thick."

Children of the patrician class either went barefoot or wore sandals. Light sandals were simply a leather sole bound on with thongs either between the toes and around the ankles, or only with thongs between the great toe and the second toe.

At times boys, and perhaps girls, wore heavy sandals made of wood and bronze. A pair in the Museum of the Villa Giulia has a jointed sole. In the same museum there are fragments of a child's sandals with small pieces of the straps that held them on the foot.

The Etruscans were a luxury-loving people, and, at their zenith in the sixth century B.C., they had sufficient wealth to gratify their desires. The seventh century had seen the building of the huge chambered tombs, decorated and brightly-painted. To attain their wealth the Etruscans had now reached out far beyond their original settlements, southward first, where they founded settlements or captured those already there. Here they formed the first of their three confederations, and established lucrative industries. Toward the end of the century they captured Rome, Ruma in the Etruscan tongue, and set over its polyglot people their own man, later known as Tarquin the Elder and the first of his race to become the king of Rome. In the sixth century, Tarquinia declined somewhat before the rising prosperity of Cerveteri and Vulci. Fabulously rich, in the sixth century B.C. Vulci had the distinction of sending to Etruscan Rome Mastarna (Servius Tullius), the man whom many regard as Rome's greatest king.

By this time Etruria's maritime strength was such that she could hold her own with the other two sea powers, Greece and Carthage, and even dispute with them the control of the western Mediterranean. And so in the sixth century the wealth that flowed into Etruria was reflected in the gold, the silver, the ivory, and the precious stones with which Etruscan gentlemen and Etruscan ladies decked their persons.

Their toilet accessories consisted largely of diadems, necklaces, bracelets, earrings, and finger rings, and since these aristocrats dressed as sumptuously for the tomb as for a social occasion, our museums have greatly profited. So fascinated are we by the riches on display in the museums, that we are apt to forget about the slave or freedwoman who must have stood before her mistress, patiently holding up a brightly polished mirror while her lady discarded necklace after necklace until she found one in her cosmetic box that suited her pleasure.

Fortunately, a nameless Etruscan painter has been less forgetful. On a funeral urn in Berlin a youthful warrior in battle dress appears; he is taking leave of a woman who stands beside him, her left hand on his shoulder, her right hand loosely clasped in his. The warrior is ready to depart. His crested helmet is on his head, his long spear rests against his left shoulder, and his bridled horse waits behind him. The warrior's person is bare of adornment. The woman, too, is plainly dressed.

Beside each figure an inscription is written. Scholars who have studied these inscriptions do not agree upon their interpretation. They do not know whether the warrior is about to go into battle or to mount his horse and ride off to the After World. Mayani's reading of the inscriptions inclines him to believe that the woman is a former slave. Now a freedwoman, she is a respected member of the family and is being entrusted with the care of the warrior's children. The modesty of the woman's attitude and of her general appearance, her long closely-fitting gown, and the absence of an attempt at adornment would seem to strengthen Mayani's feeling that the urn-painter has represented a trusted freedwoman.

The evidence is inconclusive, but it is more than likely that the Etruscan jewelry in our museums belonged to the wealthy patrician class and not to their inferiors. The slaves' revolt in Volsinia was not, of course, the direct result of distinctions in dress, but such distinctions may well have contributed their share to the unrest that was long in brewing before it broke out in the third century B.C.

Meanwhile, let us look at the collection of jewelry in the British Museum. This collection, which dates from the seventh to the second century B.C., as do other collections in museums, brings forcibly home to us the luxury of those far-off days.

Fastened to a wall are two large glass-covered cases: one contains Minoan-Mycenaean jewelry, the other Etruscan. Though centuries apart in time, the jewelry in both cases seems closely related in beauty, refinement, and craftsmanship. Crude work exists in all centuries and in all cultures, and it is not missing in either ancient Egypt, Minoan Crete, Mycenaean Greece, or Etruscan Italy, but fortunately for the reputation of ancient craftsmen most of the surviving jewelry is of exceptionally high quality.

In the Etruscan case an ivy wreath of beaten gold, fragile and delicate, a marvel of craftsmanship, seems to say to the awe-struck visitor:

"Behold, I rest here, though he who wore me has long since turned to dust."

The Etruscan case contains many other pieces of beautiful jewelry: a necklace of scarabs, a set of elaborate earrings, each three inches wide, and a remarkable gold *fibula*, or brooch, from Vulci. Elsewhere in the museum, but in a locked and closely-guarded room, a collection of gold coins is kept, each jewel-like in its perfection.

76

Other museums have their treasures: Perugia its exquisite earrings and finger rings, the Gregorian Museum of the Vatican its gold pectoral and *fibula* from the Regulini-Galassi tomb, the Louvre its extraordinarily large gold ring, mounted in a separate case, the Boston Museum of Fine Arts its exceptionally good collection of terra-cottas, and the Metropolitan in New York, which displays its Cretan and Etruscan jewelry in adjoining cases.

The Archaeological Museum in Florence and the Villa Giulia in Rome, with its famed Castellani collection, are perhaps the museums most often visited by those interested in Etruscan remains. Florence houses its collection in forty-eight rooms arranged chronologically according to the region where the finds were made, and in the pleasant Garden several tombs have been reconstructed.

The museum has one treasure so small that many a visitor may overlook it: a delicate little ring made of fine gold wire that a patrician baby may once have worn and that his heartsick mother may have left on his finger when she placed him in his coffin.

IX

Language and Literature

The Etruscan syllable MI, which was written on Larthia's silver goblets, often occurs on small, quaint-looking jugs in many of our museums. But MA and ME also occur. Single letters of the alphabet too are scattered, apparently at random, on cups and vases and similar pieces of pottery. Some one has suggested that these are not random efforts, but subtle methods of enticing young Etruscans to learn their letters.

Perhaps a small ivory tablet in the Archaeological Museum in Florence may also have been intended to make learning easy for a child. The tablet, partly broken, was found in the cemetery of Marsigliana on the Albegna River. Since the tablet is only two inches wide and three and a half inches long, with a raised rim of almost a quarter of an inch that lessens the writing space, some have thought it may have belonged not to a child but to a lady who used it for jotting down notes.

Cut into the raised rim along one side of the rectangular tablet runs an alphabet of twenty-five letters. Faint traces of a stylus—the pointed instrument used in antiquity before the pen was invented —can still be seen in the center of the tablet, to which minute fragments of wax cling. This alphabet, which also runs from right to left, is the earliest example yet found of the Phoenician-Greek letters of the seventh century B.C.

The alphabet cut into its rim leads one to believe that the tablet was really intended for a child rather than for an adult, perhaps a present to a small boy just learning his letters. If the charming little tablet belonged to a child, he was probably expected to copy the letters before him and erase them, when he made a mistake, with the blunt end of his stylus. The ivory tablet was as likely to have been a present to an aristocratic little girl as to a little boy, for many girls in this unusually enlightened period of Etruscan civilization received an education comparable to that of their brothers. The lady Vegoia is often mentioned in books about the Etruscans as an example of what might be called higher education. The lady Tanaquil, too, Tarquin's influential wife, who came with him to Rome—some say urged him to come—is also cited, because of her knowledge of mathematics, medicine, and divination.

Archaeological evidence about the education of Etruscan women is plentiful. In the museum at Volterra there is a burial-urn with the effigy of a young girl on its cover. One side of the urn is decorated with a bas-relief of a group of girls who hold open scrolls in their hands, possibly school-companions of the dead girl. The bas-relief is not an isolated example; Etruscan women are frequently depicted with open scrolls. No doubt few women reached the level of a Vegoia or a Tanaquil, though some ancient sources imply that all Etruscan women were somewhat versed in the art of divination.

Girls of the *lucumo* set may perhaps have been initiated as Tanaquil was into some of the mysteries of the Tagetic Doctrine. Tanaquil was not only skilled in sciences; she was a good housewife as well. Management of those large and stately mansions in which the *lucumo* set lived required much of a housewife, no matter how many slaves she had. Many things the daughter of the house had to learn before her marriage day: especially how to keep the fingers of her slaves too busy to make mischief, perhaps even

79

how to regulate the rhythm of the music to which a slave was flogged.

A common girl, whether serf or slave, had little to look forward to after she had put away her childish things. Education was not for her. As soon as she was old enough, she began to help her mother with household tasks, at times her father in the fields, perhaps yoked to his plow, as I once saw a woman years ago in Egypt yoked beside a water-buffalo.

If our Etruscan girl was the property of a *lucumo* household and did not prove satisfactory, she ran the risk of being flogged, unless she had a pretty face and figure that might be spoiled for further uses. In any event, she would be married as soon as she reached the necessary age for child-bearing, since this was the whole purpose and end of a woman's life.

Etruscan boys of the *lucumo* set must have had to master the rules of Tages fairly early in childhood, for they seem to have assisted, as youths, in the ritual ceremonies that played such an essential part in Etruscan life. On these occasions they wore a special dress, a white toga-like garment bordered with purple. Livy says that early in the fourth century B.C. Roman patricians began sending their sons to Etruria to be educated, presumably to Tarquinia and to Cerveteri, and, some sources hold, also to Perugia. Here they would learn the Etruscan language, which seems to have become as popular in Rome, at least for a certain length of time, as French was among English-speaking people. Roman boys may also have learned something about the Tagetic Doctrine.

An interesting Etruscan word, which Mayani has deciphered, appears on a gem that shows a boy with his abacus, or bead-frame commonly used in ancient days for calculating sums. The word is *apcar*. The ending *ar*, Mayani explains, indicates a profession or habit. One assumes that the boy is studying mathematics and that he habitually uses his abacus. (Some Japanese business men in America still do.)

The training given to boys who were not of the *lucumo* set, but whose parents belonged to the later working class must have been very unlike that of their masters. A boy would have been put to work as soon as he was old enough to help his father till the ground, care for the animals, tend the sheep, and carry out the numerous other small tasks boys still perform in the Mediterranean world. If his father was a worker in metals or precious stones, a maker of shoes, or of the false teeth held together with gold wire —on display in the museum at Tarquinia and also in the Villa Giulia—to mention only a few occupations, the boy would learn his father's trade.

The question of the mysterious Etruscan language now confronts us. Until recently, this question has been associated with the hitherto unsolved problem of the origin of the people who spoke the language. Among the three possibilities I have discussed briefly in my first chapter, the fifth-century view of Herodotus that the Etruscans came from overseas has been strengthened by two inscriptions on a decorated *stele,* or funeral monument, discovered during the last quarter of the nineteenth century on Lemnos, an island off the Anatolian coast, not far from the site of ancient Troy. The *stele,* now in the National Museum in Athens, shows in profile the face of an armed warrior. One inscription is written above and beside the warrior's head; the other on one side of the *stele.*

The language of the inscriptions, though written in archaic Greek letters, has been characterized as Etruscoid. The *stele* is not, however, an isolated document. Other inscriptions, written in the same language, have since been found on the island. All are dated in the seventh century B.C.

These finds have led scholars to assume that, if the Etruscans came from Anatolia at some early period in their history, they may have paused on Lemnos long enough to leave a foot-print before setting out, in small groups probably, for a new home.

According to Mayani, the Etruscans were originally an "Illyrian ethnic nucleus," who emigrated, possibly as early as the eleventh century B.C., from the general region of the Danube basin, passed through Greece, including the island of Lemnos, and eventually crossed the Adriatic to Italy. Several centuries later, some members of the same ethnic stock emigrated to Italy from Anatolia, where they were known as the Rasna, or Tursha. Both groups spoke the same language, but each retained certain dialectical usages. The Etruscan language is, then, in Mayani's view, essentially Illyrian, spoken by a vigorous people who, during their short day, transformed Italy.

If we accept the results of Mayani's thirty-year study, those of us who speak English should feel ourselves closely related to the ancient Etruscans, when we use such words as "lantern, cistern, tavern, ceremony, person, letter," for these are among many others Mayani has ferreted out.

The alphabet on the ivory tablet follows the order—from right to left—observed in Etruscan inscriptions, on votive statuettes in the Vatican, on sarcophagi, on funeral urns, and on other objects. But the real difficulty Etruscologists have faced in trying to decipher these inscriptions has been, so far, the lack of a Rosetta Stone, though Mayani seems to have managed without one. The inscription on that valuable slab of basalt, found near the Rosetta mouth of the Nile and now one of the treasures of the British Museum, is written in three languages: the sacred hieroglyphic, the popular demotic, and ancient Greek.

Though, up to the present, not even a bi-lingual inscription has come to light from any part of the Mediterranean world that Etruscans may have visited on their sea-faring expeditions, a surprising number of inscriptions written only in Etruscan characters have been deciphered. For example, the open scroll of the Magistrate—on the lid of his sarcophagus in the museum at Tarquinia—contains an inscription of fifty-nine words arranged in nine lines. Enough has been deciphered to reveal the name of the dead man, his father's name, and that of his grandfather and his great-grandfather. The inscription lists his various offices, religious and civic, and states that he was the author of books on divination.

Inscribed lead tablets often contain what might be called recipes for murder. The inscriptions are brief, usually addressed to one deity of the lower world, sometimes to several, as if the writer wanted to make sure that his desires would be carried out. The formula is more or less the same as those found in other Mediterranean lands; it consecrates an individual to the service of a deity or deities, apparently a way of conveying the wish that the person named will meet with a speedy death. An inscription on an Etruscan lead tablet found near Populonia, once an important town northwest of Rome, contains the curse of a freedwoman upon several persons who appear to be related to one another, possibly the family whose slave she once was.

The two longest and most important inscriptions yet found appear to be regulations that prescribe the exact form in which certain religious rituals must be carried out. In the ancient world, to deviate from exact form was dangerous, especially if one were calling upon the infernal deities for assistance.

One of these inscriptions, on a terra-cotta tile from Capua, now in the Berlin Museum, mentions by name certain deities of the lower world. The other inscription has an interesting story connected with its discovery. Toward the middle of the nineteenth century the mummy of a woman was found in Alexandria, Egypt. A traveler became interested in the mummy and brought it to Europe. Later he donated it to what is now the Archaeological Museum of Zagreb, Yugoslavia, where it was placed among other treasures from Egypt. There it remained, unexamined, until almost the close of the century. Then one day in 1892 Jacob Krall inspected the mummy's wrappings. Imagine his astonishment to discover that the wrappings were strips of linen covered with Etruscan characters.

When the strips were removed, studied, and arranged in order, they proved to be pages torn from an ancient manuscript, or roll. The script was even, and the words equally spaced and repeated so often that they fell into a pattern. The roll, known to scholars as a *liber linteus*, or linen book, is the only one of its kind that has so far been discovered. When the words on the recovered pages were counted, the text proved to be the longest on record. Today the roll is usually referred to as the Book of the Mummy.

Discounting the repetitions, the number of fairly legible words was about five hundred and thirty. The scholars who first studied the text thought it referred to the Egyptian funeral rites that the woman wished performed at her burial ceremonies. Later scholars discarded this interpretation. Many now believe it to be a religious calendar that prescribes sacrifices for specific public occasions. If this interpretation is correct, the ritual has no connection with the mummified woman.

The problem presented by the Book of the Mummy teases the imagination. One wonders who the woman was. That she was young has been determined, but not why a cloth book was torn into strips to provide wrappings for her mummy, nor how an Etruscan religious text got into Egypt.

Mayani devotes eighty-five pages of his study to the Book of the Mummy. His interest is not in the mummified woman, but in dredging from the language of the text whatever it has to disclose. His interpretation differs from those of his predecessors, who thought the text referred either to Egyptian funeral rites or to a religious calendar. "Its main subject," Mayani states at the beginning of his discussion of the Book's twelve chapters (most scholars speak of columns) "seems to be ancestor-worship." But whether the sacrifices and funeral banquets he finds prescribed at definite times and seasons refer to the woman's own ancestors or are general prescriptions Mayani does not make clear. It is interesting to learn that the various rituals prescribed include "expressions of encouragement to the dead," assuring them that their need of blood-offerings will be met. Throughout the whole Book of the Mummy, the need of blood is stressed. The second chapter of the Book contains a fragment that Mayani has translated as follows:

> *"When day begins to dawn,*
> *Slaughter a barren cow,*
> *Smite a bull of Nunthen."*

The text inscribed on the Capua Tile, the inscriptions on sarcophagi and burial-urns, the curses on the lead tablets, the archaic

Greek of the Lemnian *stele,* characterized as Etruscoid, the letters on the ivory tablet, and the lengthy inscription on the Egyptian mummy have all helped scholars in their constant efforts to decipher the Etruscan language. Additional help has come from ancient writers, both Greek and Roman, who have provided other clues: Etruscan words with a translation added, names of months, of medicinal plants, and of gods and goddesses that bear a similarity to each other, for example, *Menrva* and *Minerva.* Loan-words, such as *antenna,* yardarm, *histrio,* actor, have drifted into the Latin language. Words and roots of words that appear to be common to Etruscan and to Tuscan dialects have been analyzed. Finally, much has been learned by comparing an Etruscan formula with one in Greek or in Latin that seems to have a similar content.

A comparative method such as this was what Pallotino used in establishing the meaning of the Etruscan *mi,* equivalent to the English I or Me. Formulas on two vases, or pitchers, one in Etruscan, the other in Faliscan, which is practically archaic Latin, Pallotino explains, turned out to be "identical expressions couched in two different languages: *I am the pitcher of . . . Enoteus."*

At first the problem of the language, Linear B, once spoken in Minoan Crete, offered the same difficulties. But in 1952, after comparing the numerous clay tablets found in Crete with those of Pylos on the Greek mainland, Ventris and Chadwick were able to show that the language of the tablets from Knossos and from Pylos was a form of archaic Greek.

With neither Etruscan tablets nor literary texts to study, scholars are checked by a broad gap that can only be bridged if papyri should be found somewhere. "Such a miraculous find," writes Pallotino, "would re-echo the extraordinary discovery of an Etruscan text written on the linen wrappings of an Egyptian mummy."

If the papyri Pallotino so longs for were to contain a text that could be considered literature and that could help us understand more fully those still mysterious Etruscans and their Tagetic Doctrine, the world would join Pallotino in his rejoicing. For nothing that can be called literature has survived. Nor is there any evidence that a national literature ever existed to illuminate the Etruscan world for us as the Greek and Roman literatures have illuminated the classical world.

The lack of evidence is, however, no real argument that no literature ever existed. Greek and Roman sources contain brief references to "books" dealing with the art of divination through examination of animal entrails and from objects struck by lightning. Other "books" dealt with the regulations that controlled sacrifices, the founding of cities, even the proper division of fields, and civil and military organizations.

Mayani calls attention to a scene on the back of a mirror that shows a boy with a book open on his lap. Beside him, seated upon a higher stool, we see an older youth, his fingers on the strings of his harp, his eyes looking into the distance. His young companion, dreamy-eyed, also looks far away. Artile is his name, written clearly above his head. Mayani derives the name from the Albanian root *arti*, meaning brave.

The open book in Artile's lap resembles a small, old-fashioned double slate; the halves are held together by two clearly visible bands, set a little apart from each other. The text, Mayani admits, is "almost indistinguishable," but he has picked out the one word *iras* that has enabled him, working through Greek and Albanian, to identify the dreamy-eyed boy as Artile, the brave.

Since we can not read the text of Artile's book, we may agree with Mayani that the boy's thoughts, inspired by his book, have flown to the golden past of a by-gone day, when heroes performed deeds of valor that were long remembered in song and story. Some of these deeds Artile may have seen represented in the theater of his own day, for plays and actors were not unknown in ancient Etruria.

Drama, it is often said, is older than civilization, and one of its functions is to keep alive the memory of those who have passed from the sentient world. In Roman ceremonies the ancestors were represented by masked persons wearing the clothes that all would recognize as having belonged to the deceased. This was not pantomime; it was a serious funeral rite that originated in Etruria, where actors took a prominent part in funeral ceremonies.

Varro mentions by name an author of "Etruscan tragedies." Elsewhere other writings are referred to that were concerned with man's most agonizing problem, life beyond the grave. Pallotino thinks that parts of these religious "books" may have been composed in meter, and that the tomb inscriptions that seem to fall into a rhythmic structure "may point to the existence of *elogia,* or praises, sung in honour of important deceased persons. . . . Sacred hymns and prayers, and perhaps profane songs as well, must also have possessed a metric form." It is quite likely, then, that Varro's author composed his tragedies in meter.

Etruscan drama had its lighter side, and the actors who took part had their lighter moments. The Tomb of Inscriptions at Tarquinia, (so-called because in the various scenes painted there inscriptions often accompany the figures), shows a group of five men, three actors and two serving-men, all practically nude.

The actors are hilarious; they have had their wine, but they are still thirsty and the serving-men are bringing more. The actor in the lead, whose name is written beside him, stands with upraised arms, one lightly-booted foot on the ground, the other held high with the knee bent at a right angle to his body and the toe about to strike a small and utterly charming small dog. But the dog, with one paw uplifted, cocks his head fearlessly toward the prancing actor.

Inscribed beside the dog is a single word, *aefla,* in Etruscan letters, a word that so far as I know only Mayani has interpreted.

"*Aefla,* I have found it!" So speaks, according to Mayani, the "world's first and only talking dog."

One wonders whether the charming little dog has a part to play along with the three actors, or whether he is merely about to retrieve a lost article.

Our scant and indirect knowledge of Etruscan language and literature is partly compensated for by the wealth of our direct knowledge of the Etruscan arts. Here we are no longer looking at a mirror in which we may be gazing at the reflection of our own thought, but at what remains to us from Etruscan architecture, domestic and religious, portrait statues, goldwork, wall-paintings, and other examples of creative ability.

The question is often asked whether Etruscan art was original, and independent of Greek art. The consensus of opinion seems to be that between the eighth and seventh centuries B.C. "artistic activity developed parallel to that of other Mediterranean countries, including Greece, since all were building upon the same pre-Hellenic . . . experience."

Etruscan mythology, to which artists frequently turned for inspiration, was also built upon the "same pre-Hellenic experience."

X

Mythology and the Arts

Etruscan mythology, though borrowed almost exclusively from the Greek, had some definite characteristics of its own, among them a delightful sense of humor. Indeed, a few scholars have complained bitterly of the levity Etruscan artists exhibit in their treatment of Greek mythological themes. Others are not so much concerned about the display of such light-heartedness as they are about what they consider crass ignorance. Both criticisms are at times justified. There seems to be no reason, for example, to change the snaky-haired Medusa into a man. The artist may, of course, have confused the Etruscan demon of torture and death, Tuchulcha, also represented as having snaky locks, with the less terrible Medusa who only turned people into stone. Or perhaps the artist's inherited respect for women guided his hand.

Greek craftsmen decorated the backs of their mirrors with scenes in relief, but in Etruria toward the end of the sixth century B.C., when the mirror first came into use, this technique was soon abandoned in favor of incising, in which the Etruscan engraver was already experienced. During the next two centuries the Etruscan used varied themes, both religious and secular. In the fourth century, when Praeneste (Palestrina) became the most important center of the industry, simpler themes came into vogue, influenced, it is generally agreed, by Alexandrian poetry. Vignettes of daily life, women at their toilet, theatrical and erotic scenes with a tendency toward skepticism, and caricature, became popular. In striking contrast to these scenes were those that drew attention to the brevity of human life, seemingly never far from the Etruscan mind.

An artist with a sense of humor may be responsible for an engraving on the reverse of a mirror in Gerhard's collection which shows a group of four adults and two nude babies. Gerhard identifies the adults as Venus, Minerva, and the Dioscuri, the heavenly twins; the infants as sons of the Dioscuri. One infant sits on his father's knee, clinging fast to his left arm, his eyes fixed and staring upward. The other infant sits precariously on the open mouth of a large vase; Venus holds one hand, Minerva the other. But Minerva also supports the infant's back with her right hand. The triumphant expression on the infant's face is easily understood, and so is the complacency on the face of the first twin, obviously his father, who stands, fully relaxed, behind Minerva. The other twin is not relaxed; he looks down with concern at his own clinging son. Incidentally, both children wear the *bulla,* originally a sign of noble birth. Tages, the so-called son of Hercules, does not. Nor did Gori's Tages, the child with the plow-handles.

Children appear frequently in engravings on mirrors. The three mysterious brothers, the Kabeiri, who are sometimes interpreted as fertility gods, appear as infants on a mirror in Gerhard's collection. These triplets were worshiped in various parts of Greece, especially in Thessaly, where a secret cult existed. The initiates were forbidden to eat parsley, because the first plant sprang from the bloody head of one of the brothers, who was slain and buried by the other two at the foot of Mt. Olympus in Thessaly. The mirror engraving shows the triplets with Mercury, Minerva, and a third goddess whose only attempt at dress is an unusually beautiful necklace.

Mercury holds one infant on his left knee, Minerva seems to be extracting a second from a two-handled jar, and the goddess with the beautiful necklace carries a third child nestling comfortably in her left hand. All three infants are blessed with an abundance of curly or wavy hair. Each wears a *bulla*. The occasion is treated with the respect the critics approve of.

In another engraving Mercury holds a nude infant whose feet are shod in a pair of sandals so modern in appearance that it is hard to believe the originals were the work of a cobbler who lived thousands of years ago and who today is nameless. Perhaps his own child wore just such exquisite small sandals, and perhaps, shod in them, went to his burial place to await his transformation.

There is scarcely a well-known Greek myth that does not appear in an Etruscan guise. Scenes from the Theban cycle, especially the tragic story of Oedipus and his family, episodes from the famous Calydonian boar hunt, the labors of Hercules, Admetus and Alcestis, and many another mythological favorite occur again and again over the centuries. We are seldom able to decide whether the artist is an Etruscan who may have been trained in Greece, or a Greek working in Etruria, unless some distinctive touch betrays the artist's true background. Even then, one can be mistaken.

Greek though the theme may be, the Etruscan verve usually shines through. Hercules, bearded and carrying his club, pauses between labors to take a sup of milk from his mother's breast. In the background a lady, attired in a handsome bonnet and necklace, watches with startled eyes as his gentle-faced mother holds her nipple to the hero's eager mouth. Gerhard shows two illustrations of the nursing Hercules, each engraved on the back of a bronze mirror.

In each engraving the "mother" is Juno, not Alcmene, as the myth is usually told. Gerhard thinks the artist may have followed an unknown Etruscan version, which may certainly be true. Or we may have here a flagrant instance of Etruscan ignorance of Greek mythology. Mayani calls attention to a legend in Diodorus Siculus which states that Juno upon one occasion gave her breast to Hercules. "In Etruria there used to be a fine group by a Greek sculptor," Mayani adds, "which is now preserved in the Vatican and which represents this very scene. . . . An Etruscan engraver could have inferred from this that Juno was the demi-god's mother." That Hercules may be seeking immortality is Mayani's interpretation, based upon his reading of the inscription on the mirror.

Hercules must have been a favorite of Etruscan women, since details of his adventures occur often in the mirror-engravings. Some are amusing, even ridiculous, others are serious. In most of them he is easily distinguished by his lion-skin, which he wears usually knotted by its front paws around his neck and hanging down his back, or by his club. In two engravings that are supposed to show him as a newborn infant, his identity tokens do not appear. Both show a woman half-reclining on a couch, fully clothed except for her right breast, an infant (really an adolescent) asleep on her left arm. Nothing is visible except his head and that is covered with such a luxuriant crop of hair that it has to be restrained by a fillet.

In the first engraving a male figure in a tunic and wearing a kind of Phrygian cap stands near the foot of the couch. Between the thumb and forefinger of his right hand he holds a small, squat-bellied object that resembles a medicine bottle which he seems to be showing to the woman on the couch. She, in her turn, seems to be showing him a strange instrument something like the forceps I saw in the National Museum in Naples. The doctor, for, judging by a similar figure in the second engraving, that is who he must be, looks non-committal; Alcmene, to give the mother her correct name, smiles faintly at him. Neither one looks at the sleeping infant. The place where the birth has occurred is obviously Thebes, and the mother's name must be Alcmene, for under her couch the well-known figure of the Theban sphinx appears.

In the second representation the place of the sphinx is taken by a female figure, and the identity of the doctor is assured, because he holds in his hand, instead of a bottle, the caduceus, or staff entwined with serpents, the constant insignia of Aesculapius, the legendary father of medicine.

In another illustration from Gerhard Hercules is displaying his son to the great god Tinia. Except that this child is equipped with a pair of wings, he might easily be taken for the earth-born Tages. Tinia, heavily bearded, his hair meticulously coiffed, and robed in an embroidered gown, holds loosely grasped in one hand five sharply-pointed thunderbolts—the usual tradition gives him three. Two women attend him: they are dressed in the same fashion.

Gerhard also represents Hercules embracing Minerva, while beside him stands another male figure upon whose shoulder a nude female, sound asleep, rests her carefully-dressed head.

Judging from the elaborate coiffures to be seen in mirror-engravings, hair-dressing, especially for women, must have become almost a fine art. In most instances, the styling is excellently adapted to the shape of the face. One young girl is shown wearing a pony-tail.

In Etruscan art partiality for the nude male figure soon came to include the nude female figure. A mirror-engraving in Gerhard's collection and reproduced in Mayani, who calls the scene "La belle Helene," shows Menelaus and the goddess Aphrodite completely nude. Paris and Helen are almost too clothed. Not even their feet are visible, for both wear costumes that touch the ground. Aphrodite wears earrings, two necklaces, and a bracelet on each wrist. Menelaus is the center of attention; he stands between Aphrodite and Helen, who with one hand resting lightly on his arm seems to be restraining him. No one pays any attention to Paris, the only seated member of the group, a courtesy to the newly-arrived traveler from distant Troy, perhaps.

"The comedy of the situation," Mayani explains, "lies in the glance exchanged between Venus and Paris. . . . they are as thick as thieves and the understanding between them is perfect. These are true pantomime effects, which must have given great pleasure to their Etruscan beholders."

The scene, Mayani appears to think, was inspired by a mimetic performance in which Menelaus appeared on the point of leaving when Aphrodite arrived, bringing Paris along to claim his prize for awarding her the golden apple. Helen, innocent of her future, tries to persuade her husband not to leave when visitors have just come to the palace. The situation has its comic relief, but one wonders whether in even a late period of Etruscan life the goddess of love would be represented in a spectacle as completely nude. The mirror-engraver may, of course, have been influenced by the current Roman fashion of representing both male and female mime-players in the nude. Before the end of the third century B.C. the performance of mimes, generally indecent, became the most popular feature at the spring flower-festival, the Floralia. By this time in both Greece and Rome the taste for realism had outgrown all previous restrictions. Under the Empire mimes practically monopolized the stage. People of all ranks, high and low, flocked to see them. Caricatures were particularly admired.

Etruscan craftsmen did not confine their treatment of mythological subjects to engravings on the backs of mirrors. Their fingers were equally skillful in adapting their themes to their material, a tomb wall to be frescoed, a bronze or terra-cotta statue in the round, or a temple to be decorated in the bright colors the Etruscans loved. Though Etruria depended upon Greek art for its general effect, her artists became in their turn a "center of influence for . . . western arts."

Bronze cosmetic boxes (*cistae*), so dear to the heart of an Etruscan lady, offered a somewhat different field to the engraver. The round shape of the mirror provided him with space for the sweep of a wing; the rectangular, square, or cylindrical cosmetic box encouraged him to present continuous scenes of a single adventure, such as that of the Argonauts on the handsome fourth-century Ficcorini box made in Praeneste. A marriage-gift, the inscription reads, from a wealthy lady to her daughter, large enough to hold all the bride's possessions: her jewels, her mirrors, her paints and brushes, whatever she needs to make herself beautiful in the eyes of her husband.

The exterior of the box does not exhibit nude young ladies, but Jason's ship, the Argo, pulled up on shore, and one of his companions carrying a pail to find water and bring it back to the ship. The youth meets with an adventure which nearly costs him his life, but like the hero he is, he overcomes the king of the savage land, ties him to a tree, and returns triumphant to his shipmates.

The Ficcorini coffer, named after its discoverer, is today one of the treasures of the Villa Giulia in Rome. The handles of these cosmetic boxes offered excellent opportunities to the craftsmen. The handle of this particular marriage-gift is composed of two bronze figures, who stand on the lid, each with his outstretched arm resting upon his companion's. Sometimes a handle shows two warriors carrying a dead companion horizontally between them.

Mythological themes, though they found their proper home in the minor arts, were not wanting in the major arts. The Etruscan temple, hampered somewhat when it did not imitate the Greek temple with its pediment, mounted its deities high on the roof where all could see them. The frieze that encircled the upper part of the temple may well have been used for decorative purposes, but since an Etruscan temple was built of wood or bricks on a foundation of stone, today nothing remains except a few lower courses of stone. These are naturally valuable, because they trace the ground plan of the sanctuary.

Vitruvius, the Roman architect and engineer who lived in the time of the Emperor Augustus, states that an Etruscan temple was rectangular—its width only a little less than its length—with a deep portico and colonnades. Three cells, each dedicated to a different god, occupied the rear of the temple. The roof, like the framework, was of wood with a broad overhang. Brilliantly painted in red and blue and green, decorated with groups of statuary, or a single beautiful head sometimes fitted into a delicately carved wooden shell, an Etruscan temple reflected the joyful exuberance of Etruscan life. No Puritan restraint hampered either architect or painter.

Recent excavations at Veii have brought out the supports which were used for the statues of Apollo and of Hercules that stood on the roof of the temple there. The scene is thought to have represented the dispute between the god and the hero over the sacred golden hind, the property of Apollo's sister Diana. Hercules, after pursuing the hind for a year, had finally caught it. When he refused to hand over his trophy, Apollo took his sister's part. The dispute was settled in Hercules's favor.

The famous winged horses in the museum at Tarquinia once ornamented the façade of a third-century temple there. Harnessed to the chariot of a god, these eager-eyed, spirited horses are ready to take to the air the instant they hear their master's word. Surely no less majestic a god than Tinia himself should have the privilege of guiding them to heaven's portal.

The first impulse toward realistic portraiture in which later Etruscan art excelled is found in the canopic burial-urns from Chiusi and in the portrayal of deceased persons on the lids of their sarcophagi. The mythological figures in high relief on the sides of the sarcophagi also tend to be realistic. Realism occurs in representations of funeral scenes, banquets, athletic games, and dances painted on the walls of the tombs.

Alain Hus in his book on the Etruscans has called attention to the vigorous realism of the bronze warriors of the fifth century. One of them, belonging to the second half of the century, he calls an "astonishing work." He notes particularly "the undulation of the movements, the sense of the instantaneous, the gesture of recoil before attack."

In this connection it is interesting to learn that today the famous Orator in the Archaeological Museum in Florence, long thought to have been Roman, has been assigned to Etruscan realism.

Southern Etruria gave rise, from the fourth century on, to what has been called "absolute realism," the photographic exactitude of the unlovely features of old age, with no attempt to portray the informing spirit within. An example of this realism is shown in the burial-urn from Volterra with the aged couple resting on its lid. "So diabolically real," writes Hus, "is the face of the old woman that some have imagined seeing in her, not the companion of the dead man, but Death herself, surreptitiously gliding toward the man, hovering about him."

At this period in Etruscan life, Death was indeed hovering over these people who had risen so high, but who were now slipping back, step by step, before the advancing might of Rome, yet were unable to unite their own discordant elements, even in the face of imminent disaster. They had lost the south; they had lost Rome; they were almost back where they had started, in the still fertile area between the Tiber and the Arno. Tuchulcha was hovering over all of them.

Caught up in the general feeling of uneasiness, the artists of the period, though they continue to revel in Greek myth, seem to have chosen mythological scenes of massacre and of wanton destruction. Death feeds upon blood and, unsatisfied, demands more. Polyneices and Eteocles, the sons of wretched Oedipus, king of Thebes, quarrel and slay each other; Priam's daughter, Polyxena, is sacrificed on her grave, that Achilles in the next world may have his promised bride; in this strange atmosphere the Etruscans move, almost like dream-walkers, toward their destined end.

Mayani, in his chapter on mythological subject matter, from which I have drawn rather freely, reproduces the well-known parting scene between Admetus and Alcestis. The scene, painted with gruesome realism, occurs on an Etruscan vase which I have not seen. Nor do I know its date. Not that either matters; the artist's painting is our chief interest.

Admetus, king of Thessaly, has been told that on a certain day he is destined to die, unless some one volunteers to die in his stead. His beloved wife, Alcestis, offers her life for his. He refuses. Quietly but firmly she argues with him. His death will not benefit either her or his people; her death will. One of the most moving scenes in Euripides's drama, *Alcestis,* is the farewell between Alcestis and her young children; it occurs just before Alcestis goes to her death.

The Etruscan artist has chosen the farewell scene between Admetus and Alcestis; in his painting, husband and wife stand facing each other in a last embrace. Behind Admetus stands the hideous Tuchulcha. Under his left arm he holds a spotted snake, partly uncoiled. Grinning horribly, he holds out in his right hand another

97

spotted snake, its hissing head only inches away from the king's neck.

An equally horrifying figure stands behind Alcestis; he has the face of a startled gorilla, its ugliness accentuated by a sparse beard and tufts of hair falling over his forehead. Armed with a heavy broad-axe, he stands ready to strike.

If these are the creatures the aged woman, sculptured on the lid of her burial-urn, expects to encounter in the After World, it is no wonder that she herself looks like death.

The difference between Etruscan and Greek artistic expression, according to Pallotino, lies in the fact that Etruria did not develop a tradition and Greece did, invigorated by fresh artistic breezes sweeping in from her new colonies in Sicily and southern Italy. From the moment Etruscan craftsmen welcomed their Greek neighbors into their studios, their own artistic efforts in almost every field except in portraiture were destined to drop beneath the surface and flow quietly underground until medieval Europe should need the Etruscan view of reality.

Though the Etruscans may not have developed, as the Greeks did, a genuine tradition of artistic expression, in one field, that of the dance with musical accompaniment, they distinguished themselves. They danced in pairs, they danced singly, they danced to placate angry gods, they danced to please their ancestors, but the dance as a form of worship seems to have been unknown to them.

XI

Music, Dancing, and Sports

The Etruscans and the Greeks had a common musical background inherited from pre-Hellenic days. Among both peoples singing and dancing played as important a part as it did among the ancient Hebrews. The Old Testament relates that Saul's daughter, leaning out of an upper window, saw King David "leaping and dancing before the Lord; and she despised him in her heart." Overjoyed when the youthful David returned after slaying the Philistines, the women of Israel came out to meet him, "singing and dancing." On this occasion the women played on "tabrets" and "answered one another as they played."

Music was woven into the very texture of Greek life. Unlike the Romans who never acquired a passion for music, the Greeks included the study of music in their educational system. The hero Achilles, sulking in his tent on the Trojan shore, whiled away his time making music on his lyre, and Agamemnon, the commander-in-chief of the Greek expedition, thought none the worse of him. Harvest songs and vintage songs, marriage songs and dirges were part of man's daily life. The Italian country folk had their songs, too, but no serious Roman would ever have agreed with Plato, that music could influence a man's character.

From the very beginning of the Pythian Games, which long

stood as high in the estimation of ancient Greece as the Olympic Games in the modern world, musical contests were held along with athletic contests. Today, of the four great games, the Pythian, the Nemean, the Isthmian, and the Olympic, only the strictly athletic Olympic Games have survived.

Plato, in his imaginary Eutopia, would not include in the education of the young certain types of music, particularly the Ionian and the Lydian modes, as too effeminate and as tending toward the orgiastic, yet he did not object to Phrygian music and Aristotle did. There is sufficient evidence, however, both literary and archaeological, to warrant us in assuming that Lydian and Phrygian music found a congenial atmosphere in ancient Etruria. So far as we know, Etruscan musicians were uninhibited. This was not true everywhere in Greece. The Argive Greeks passed laws that were intended to preserve their music from outside influences. The Spartans, so it is said, enforced their Dorian mode with unparalleled severity. Those who were rash enough to introduce innovations in the solemn and grave Dorian music were punished, and their offending instruments destroyed.

The musical instruments we hear most of in the ancient world are the wind instruments, the trumpet and the flute, and the stringed instruments, the lyre, characterized by strings of equal length, the harp with strings of unequal length, and the cithara, an elaborated form of the lyre. The Greek tragic poets thought that the Etruscans invented the trumpet. Pallotino feels that whether the Etruscans actually invented the trumpet or not, it fulfilled so important a part in military ceremonials and possibly in some religious ceremonials that it must have eventually been manufactured in Etruscan workshops.

The trumpet came in two models, a straight bronze tube, or *tuba,* sometimes curved at one end, and the curved model, the *cornu,* or horn. The Romans adopted the trumpet in both forms. The Etruscans also had percussion instruments, such as castanets, which some authorities think the Moors introduced into Europe.

Since it is known that the ancient Greeks used castanets, it is likely that the Etruscans took a fancy to them, as they did to many other things in use among their eastern neighbors. Castanets should have had as strong an appeal to an Etruscan dancer as to a Spanish dancer of today.

Among the Greeks, the music of the flute, or double pipes, accompanied the orgiastic ceremonies in honor of Dionysus, the god of wine, in which the women whipped themselves into a frenzy, tearing young animals apart and drinking their blood. Compared with these orgies, the so-called "frenetic" movements of the professional Etruscan dancer seem merely to portray the lust for living that, at least in their zenith, distinguished these joyous, carefree aristocrats from other Mediterranean people.

From the predominance of the flute in Etruscan paintings and on reliefs, it seems fair to believe that the music of the flute accompanied almost all activities of Etruscan life; to its notes, probably muted upon occasion, the baker kneaded his dough, the scourger modulated his blows upon the back of a disobedient slave, and animals stole out from their dens. Indeed, so frequently do ancient authors allude to the Etruscan flute that it was probably the national instrument.

Etruscan paintings show the flute being played alone or with a lyre or zither (cithara). Since we cannot hear the melody, we must needs be content with what we are told, that the sweet and nobler notes drawn from the strings of the lyre or the zither soften the passionate music of the flute, both tempering the blare of the horn whenever it joins the other two.

In Greece the victory of the lyre over the flute comes to us in the form of a myth, the well-known story of the contest between the goddess Athena and the satyr Marsyas, Athena with her lyre and Marsyas with his flute. After each had played a few notes, they exchanged instruments. But when Athena saw how ugly she was with her cheeks puffed out, she tossed away the instrument, and decreed that Marsyas should forfeit his life for having dared to enter into a contest with her.

The frequent appearance of wind instruments in Etruscan paintings, to the exclusion of the lyre, may point to the development of instrumental music accompanied by gesture rather than by song. Gesture would lead to mime, and Livy assures us that the mime was popular in Etruria.

Statuettes of masked comedy-actors have been found in some of the tombs, and these discoveries, added to the increasing influence of Greek drama upon the Mediterranean world, makes it probable that dialogue may soon have gained a place on the early Etruscan stage. In Israel, the women "answered one another while they played."

Since musical instruments were sometimes played together, as the paintings show, it would be interesting to know whether the Etruscans ever showed any inclination to develop orchestral music, to be played alone, or to accompany their dancers. If the Etruscans brought with them from Lydia the knowledge of orchestral music, it might have blossomed, if not for themselves, then for the later Roman Empire, where wind instruments of many kinds were developed, perhaps an inheritance from the Etruscans.

That young Etruscans, as well as young Greeks, learned the art of music, either by rote or by ear, is attested by both archaeological and literary evidence. The youth who sits beside the boy Artile holds a five-stringed instrument upright on his knee. He, too, is in as deep a reverie as his younger companion. Either the mirror-engraver has not reproduced accurately the musical instrument, or we are looking at an Etruscan variation of the usual Greek lyre which in its earliest form had four strings and later seven. This lyre has five vertical strings.

Another engraving shows the god Apollo with a regulation four-stringed lyre, which the artist has obviously added to the scene (along with an unusually large swan) by way of identifying the god. In Greece the seven-stringed lyre was in use in the fifth century B.C. That it was also in use at approximately the same time in Etruria may be surmised from its appearance in a wall-painting (Tomb of the Two Arches) in Tarquinia.

The five-stringed lyre Artile's musician friend holds may be one of those instances of carelessness that make some critics so unhappy, or a five-stringed lyre may really have existed in Etruria. One of the most ancient of stringed instruments, its origin has been traced back to 1700 B.C. among the Semitic races. The lyre was popular in Egypt, Asia Minor, and Greece, and eventually made its way in Etruscan hands to Rome. The modern guitar is its legitimate descendant.

The tomb paintings show both male and female dancers. Though some of the books say that Etruscans danced in couples, this is not strictly true; they dance facing each other, but never in couples, as the history of the dance shows. Couple dances were late in developing, and for various reasons. The male dances for the female, and the female for the male; the ancient code of morals forbade all else.

The tombs of Tarquinia have yielded most of our information about the Etruscan dance. Additional information comes from Chiusi. According to Mary Johnstone's careful study, twenty-one of these tomb scenes have been described in detail, many of them by Dennis and by others who saw them before they were removed. Eight belong to the sixth century, thirteen to the fifth. Seventeen come from Tarquinia, four from Chiusi. These are Mary Johnstone's figures. She also tells us that the "dance as a subject of tomb decoration is confined within the last half of the sixth century and the first half of the fifth."

Since the language of early man was inadequate to express his emotions, he had to vent them in physical movement, fling out his arms, beat his head, run, and leap high into the air. Out of his inadequacy, then, gesture and dancing were born, not as mere physical movement, but movement with a meaning attached. Many, including Mary Johnstone, think that man's need for food, and the urge to do something about it, when the seed he has planted seems in danger of fruition, lie at the root of the religious dance.

The Etruscan dance, as we know it, had advanced far beyond that primitive stage. The dances illustrated in the tomb frescoes of the sixth century contain no hint, in Johnstone's opinion, of an earlier religious stage. There are no processions, with musical accompaniment, in honor of a god, no Bacchic frenzies comparable to those of the fifth century in Greece.

A fresco in the so-called Tomb of the Leopards at Tarquinia, belonging to the end of the sixth century B.C., shows us an interesting dance being performed. The fresco fills the simulated pediment of a temple, presented in the usual triangular shape. A short curved column in the apex of the triangle is guarded on either side not by leopards but by a couchant lioness with protuberant dugs and switching tail.

The rectangular space below the two animals, whose spots caused their mis-naming, is filled with a two-handled funeral jar, decorated with a garland, and two male musicians who, like the lionesses above their heads, face each other. The musician to the left holds a lyre, his companion a flute. Both men are fully clothed and shod in boots with upcurled toes.

On either side of the two musicians three dancers are shown, one a woman who dances alone, the other two, a man and a slender young girl, who dance facing each other but never touching. The woman who dances alone wears a bordered *tutulus,* or high cap, a transparent polka-dotted dress, a blue cloak lined with red, that seems to swing from her shoulders, and long-toed boots, low in front, high in back. She wears a necklace, armlets, and circular ornaments above her ears.

The two dancers on the opposite side of the funeral jar seem to be gesturing to each other, the girl responding to the man with the usual gesture—two fingers folded down—that is sometimes interpreted as efficacious in warding off the evil eye. The girl also wears a transparent dress, but without a cloak; the man, sturdy and young, is completely nude. Some one has called this dance an Etruscan version of the twist.

Mary Johnstone calls particular attention to the disregard, in Etruscan illustrations of the dance, of *chiastico,* or "co-ordinated grouping in which one upper limb is in the forward position when the lower limb of the same side is in the backward position." If this principle is disregarded, she explains, no "harmonious rhythm" of the body is possible. Here the dancing girl advances her left arm and her left leg together; *chiastico* requires one member to be in the opposite position.

The girl's dancing partner is also drawn with a disregard of *chiastico*. "If the artist had elevated the left foot instead of the right and had brought it forward this would have been an elegant dancer." As portrayed in the fresco, the beauty of rhythmical movement is completely lacking.

The Tomb of Hunting and Fishing, also in Tarquinia, contains a fresco in which the principle of *chiastico* is not disregarded. The dances, unfortunately much defaced, were painted on the walls of the small chamber that led into the main room with its scenes of men and boys actively engaged in hunting and fishing.

In the anteroom the dancers are correctly drawn; their movements are rhythmical, vigorously alive, but with a restraint that is truly Greek. The dancers are nude; in sheer gaiety of spirit they have tossed their mantles on the branches of the trees in the olive grove where they are dancing. The artist has not quite mastered his technique; he still clings to the old frontal position of the upper part of the body with the legs in profile, but he has learned to turn the head, to place the feet in the proper rhythmical position, and to observe the principle of *chiastico*.

The frescoes of the fifth-century tombs have true dances to show us: the Tomb of the Triclinium from the first half of the century and the Tomb of Francesca Giustiniani from the middle of the century. Both tombs are in the Tarquinia area. The fresco from the first tomb shows men and women dancing in the open air. Birds peck at the olives, a squirrel darts along a branch, and a cat prowls below. The women wear flowered dresses, voluminous cloaks, and ankle-high boots; sometimes they play with the ends of long scarves, or decorate the bushes with them. The men drape mantles around their shoulders; on their feet are the usual ankle boots, which some take to be strapped sandals.

Two of these dancers are reproduced so often that they have become famous. One is a man, the other a woman. Both are filled with the exuberant joy of living. Though we still see the frontal body and the profile limbs, here we pay little attention to them, so instinct with happiness the dancers seem. Some think these are professional dancers; others prefer to see them as guests at a lawn party given by an Etruscan nobleman who will afterwards have them painted on the walls of his tomb that he may enjoy them in the After World.

The two famous dancers are among the lines shown approaching their host's banquet table. There the nobleman awaits his guests, for surely that is what they are, in the happy, carefree days before Etruria felt the might of Rome.

So little remains of the decorations from the Tomb of Francesca Giustiniani that one must depend, largely, upon the description Dennis has left. The inclusion in the fresco of horses, other animals, and men caused Dennis to imagine a hunting scene. Mary Johnstone calls attention to the excellent drawing of a left hand, superior to what earlier artists had achieved. The hand is that of a young man who holds a rod with a curved, hook-like piece set in near the top; its true significance has never, to my knowledge, been satisfactorily explained.

A fitting close to the tomb representations of the Etruscan dance and its performers might be the little dancer George Dennis fell in love with the first time he saw her, as Mary Johnstone says, dancing "amongst the ghostly shreds of her companions," there on the wall of Francesca's tomb. I can do no better than to quote Mary Johnstone again: "She is the sweetest and the simplest of all the frescoed Etruscan women . . . the bubble dancing on the stream, the flower swaying in the breeze, the butterfly hovering above the flower-bed."

No one knows the little dancer's name.

There were many kinds of dances: courting dances, round dances for the women, martial dances for the men, and funeral dances, such as form a part of all early cultures. In Etruria, musicians had their guilds, and dancers theirs, but whether the same guild served both performers we do not know. Nor do we know whether women belonged to the men's guild or had guilds of their own.

Every culture has had its sacred ritual dance performed upon stated occasions to please the dead ancestors. At the Vlach festival for the dead three young men and three girls dance the *kolo,* the dance of death. During the performance, elderly women sometimes go into a trance and fall to the ground. The men of the village then dance in a ring around the unconscious women, who are believed to be in communication with the dead. To revive the women, if other means have failed—guns are frequently fired—water from a nearby river is brought and the women are washed in it.

For the most part, the frescoes from Tarquinia display happy, joyous dances. The great sarcophagi of the nobles and the hermetic urns are decorated with funeral dances and ritual processions led by a musician, or by events of daily life, usually connected with the life of the deceased. Funeral dances are solemn, the gestures of the mourners (sometimes hired for the occasion) are formal and restrained, the music oftener that of the flute rather than of the lyre. Both men and women participate, especially in the processions; the men at times with one hand extended toward the bier, the other, palm down, on the head; the women with unbound hair and both hands covering the face.

Many of these scenes include an altar, not for worship of a god, but for worship of an ancestor. Mary Johnstone states emphatically that she has found no evidence that the Etruscans used the dance-form in the worship of a god, as the Greeks did, but always in ancestor worship. This is not so strange as it appears; the Etruscans have clung to their inherited ways and the Greeks have not. For the Indo-European believed, as de Coulanges has shown, that ancestors became gods, that they were sheltered beneath the hearthstone, and that the hearthstone became, in course of time, the altar.

Mary Johnstone has also studied dance scenes on Etruscan vases, bas-reliefs, bronzes, and mirrors. She has made the interesting discovery of a chain-dance pictured on one of the earliest and probably the "most primitive, of the painted vases found in Etruria." The chain-dance, as most visitors to Greece know, is still performed by the women of Megara at Easter-time. Minoan Crete also knew the chain-dance, or ring-dance, as it is sometimes called. There it was danced in honor of a god. Its presence on a vase in Etruria forms another link, as Mary Johnstone notes, in the evidence pointing to an Eastern origin for the Etruscan people.

A processional dance shown on a silver bucket in the Archaeological Museum in Florence may represent warriors paying their last respects to one of their number, possibly their chief, whose funeral they are attending. The procession is moving toward an altar; it includes men on horseback, men leading animals, and women carrying baskets on their heads. Obviously a sacrifice is to be performed. The dancing men are arranged in pairs, one behind the other; the forward member leaps into the air. Knees bent, both feet off the ground, he reminds one of Hitler's ill-timed "dance of joy." The purpose of the sacrifice is controversial; it may be to honor the dead man, or to placate a god, or it may be merely preliminary to a war-expedition.

In 364 B.C. Etruscan dancers, for the first time, as Livy tells us, were summoned to Rome. A plague had fallen upon the city, and expiation ceremonies were needed to placate the angry gods, at whose bidding the evil had fastened upon the city. Before summoning the Etruscans, from what city Livy does not say, the Romans had tried to placate the gods by holding war games and athletic contests in the Circus. Then they introduced *ludi,* games, or in modern speech, shows. Evidently the *ludi* did not quell the angry gods, for the plague continued unabated.

Finally the Romans summoned the Etruscans, possibly from nearby Veii. For when the Gauls, streaming down earlier from the north, terrorizing all Etruria, had crossed the Tiber to attack Rome, the Romans had sent their gods to Veii to prevent the Gauls from capturing them. The Veientes had had no choice but to give sanctuary to the Roman gods, for only one year before the Gauls invaded Etruria the Romans had tricked Veii into surrender and made her a subject city.

The Etruscan dancers came, bringing their flutes; they danced, probably in the Circus, "not without grace," Livy says grudgingly, but they did not accompany their dance with songs or gestures. Out of this special performance, again according to Livy, grew Roman drama.

The graceful movements of the Etruscan dancers, who may have put on a mimetic show of some kind with masks, evidently dispelled the anger of the gods, for the plague left Rome.

The Etruscans were fond of games and sports. Since the Lydians are said to have invented the game of dice, they probably carried the "bones" with them in their wanderings, perhaps teaching their use to Greece as they passed through. On a large amphora (two-handled jar) in the Gregorian Museum, Achilles and Ajax are shown with their hands held out and fingers extended as if they were playing with the *astragali,* or knuckle-bones, which we call dice. Beside each player is written in Attic Greek the number he has just announced: four for Achilles, three for Ajax.

Livy mentions, skeptically, that in 437 B.C. when Fidenae, a Roman colony, revolted to Veii and Rome sent ambassadors to ask why they had defected, an ambiguous expression that Lars Tolumnius, the *lucumo* of Veii, tossed off while engaged in a game of dice, caused the death of the Roman envoys.

In the same Tomb of the Inscriptions at Tarquinia where we saw the three actors and their dog, there was another fresco; it was badly defaced but, on the evidence of early drawings, it seems to have shown two nude men playing a game of dice. Unfortunately, no dice are visible on the table between them, yet the position of their hands in these early drawings seems to indicate that they were engaged in some such game. Whether the Lydians invented dice or not, six-sided cubes much like our own have been found in the tombs of Egypt, in the ruins of Babylon, and in Etruscan tombs.

The difficulty that has faced Etruscologists and others who have studied the Etruscan dice is that the Etruscans, instead of using dots, incised a word on each face, and the meaning of these words scholars have not agreed upon. Transliterated into their Latin equivalents and arranged alphabetically, the six words are: CI, HUθ, MAX ŚA, θU, ZAL. At first sight the problem seems easy: six faces and six words, but how were they to be arranged to form a sequence of one to six?

Until Mayani's book appeared in 1961, the conventional view was as follows: 1=θU; 2=ZAL; 3=CI; 4=ŚA; 5=MAX; 6=HUθ. From this interpretation, scholars drew some comfort; they could be sure of the first six digits in the numerical scale, an important forward step in deciphering Etruscan numbers. This conventional view, widely accepted, Mayani has now challenged.

Based upon the linguistic evidence, Mayani's sequence is as follows: 1=MAX; 2=θU; 3=CI; 4=HUθ; 5=ŚA; 6=ZAL. In both views 3=CI. Since the evidence Mayani presents to justify his sequence occupies an entire chapter and is difficult to summarize, I have taken the liberty of borrowing his diagram from page eighty-three and the diagram of the conventional view from page seventy-one. In both diagrams 3, or CI, occupies the same position. On a modern die, the dots on the six sides, numbered from one to six, are always so placed that the sum of the dots on opposite sides equals seven. To this rule the conventional view conforms; Mayani's does not seem to.

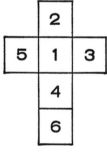

Mayani's diagram

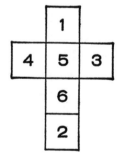

Conventional diagram

Though dicing was a favorite game with the Etruscans, they also indulged in such active sports as boxing, prize-fights, and wrestling. Illustrations of these and other sports are shown on tomb paintings and on funeral urns. The Tomb of the Augurs at Tarquinia shows a pair of naked wrestlers; they seem engaged in testing each other's strength, as with heads nearly touching, they grasp each other's wrists with such force that their muscles bulge.

That the Etruscans also enjoyed horse-racing and gladiatorial contests can be seen by the enthusiasm shown in the paintings and reliefs, where spectators watch with strained attention. The gladiatorial contests, an outgrowth of earlier human sacrifice at the tombs that the dead might have their meed of blood, may have originated in southern Etruria. Here the Romans first saw these contests and eagerly espoused them. In Campania the dead gladiators were dragged away by the man disguised as Tuchulcha, the winged demon of the Etruscan underworld.

A fresco in the Tomb of the Augurs illustrates one Etruscan game that violates all modern ideas of fair play. The painting shows two contestants: one man wears a mask, the other has his head in a sack tied fast around his neck. The masked man holds in leash an excited hound; the hooded man, naked except for a loin-cloth, is armed with a heavy club.

In this savage game the masked man urges the leashed dog to spring at his hooded antagonist and try to bring him down. The artist has chosen to represent the moment after the hooded man has already been bitten several times, for blood is streaming from his wounds. To our eyes, man and dog are unfairly matched, because the hooded wretch has no chance of escaping, unless by a lucky hit he clubs the hound to death.

Some have thought that this unpleasant scene does not represent a game but a human sacrifice, possibly at a funeral. Whatever its interpretation, such a fresco could easily engender the feeling that the Etruscans were as hardened to the sight of human suffering as the Romans were. We must remember, though, that in the ancient world compassion was not a quality to be cultivated. Indeed, one would not go far wrong in holding that compassion, as we understand it, did not even exist. The over-riding necessity was, until very late, the preservation of one's ancestors. Otherwise the family, as such, would cease to exist, and no misfortune could be greater. If, then, what has been called a game was, in reality, the shedding of blood to maintain the flickering life of the dead, the savage game shown in the fresco can be understood.

PART THREE
THE BRONZE AGE

"... a brazen race. ... terrible and strong. ...
Their armour was of bronze. ..."

HESIOD, *Works and Days*

XII

The City of the She-Wolf

The traditional account of the people we call Romans is that Aeneas, who belonged to the junior branch of the royal house of Troy, escaped with his aged father, his young son, and a band of loyal followers from burning Troy and finally reached Italy. There Aeneas's son eventually founded the Latin city of Alba Longa. In the long list of Aeneas's descendants, Romulus and his twin brother Remus appear in the fifteenth generation as the reputed grandsons of Numitor, who was at that time the Latin king of Alba Longa.

Earlier, Numitor with his brother Amulius had ruled jointly over Alba Longa. But Amulius soon proposed a division: one brother to possess the Trojan spoils, the other to possess the kingdom. Numitor chose the kingdom. Later, Amulius became jealous of his brother, turned against him, and seized the kingdom. When Numitor's daughter came of marriageable age, her uncle, fearing the girl might have children, used his power to force her to become a Vestal Virgin.

The new king's precautions were in vain; his niece broke her vow of chastity and confessed that she was with child. She was arrested and flung into prison. There she bore twin boys, each of surpassing beauty. Questioned, she said their father was Mars, the god of war. Alarmed and fearful of losing his kingdom if he allowed the twins to live, Amulius had them put into a basket and set afloat in the Tiber. But the river was in flood, and the twins' basket drifted ashore near a fig tree. There a wolf found the infants and suckled them until a shepherd discovered their plight and took them into his home.

To commemorate the story, some time during the Etruscan occupation of Rome, a bronze statue, cast in the shape of a she-wolf nursing two human infants, was set up on the new temple on the Capitoline Hill, which according to tradition was built by the Tarquins. Livy says that in the third century B.C. two Roman officials ordered a similar bronze statue set up near the fig tree. Today a replica of the famous she-wolf and the infants she saved from death stands on the Campidoglio in Rome.

As usually happens in such folk tales, the part played by the wicked uncle came to the ears of the rightful king, who had the twins brought to the palace in Alba Longa and the wicked uncle disposed of. For a time the reunited family lived happily together —until the twins grew into young manhood and decided they would establish themselves in places of their own choosing, preferably nearer the Tiber.

When Romulus and Remus left their grandfather's kingdom to choose a new location, groups of eager adventurers followed them. Two of the hills near the Tiber appeared suited to their purposes, and so Romulus with his men climbed the Palatine, and Remus with his men climbed the Aventine. Legend adds that twelve vultures immediately flew over the Palatine, while only six flew over the Aventine. Plutarch, who tells the whole story, is loath to accept this easy solution; he says cautiously that some people think Romulus cheated. However that may be, Romulus chose the Palatine and Remus had to be content with the Aventine.

In ancient days, the change from one site to another without incurring the anger of the deified dead was a risky procedure. Aeneas, the twins' remote ancestor, had brought with him his father and his father's gods. Neither Romulus nor Remus could do this. Plutarch and Dionysius of Halicarnassus relate that Romulus, in his quandary, applied to the Etruscans in Tarquinia for information as to the proper rites he should follow to induce the deified dead of Alba Longa to accept a new home.

Romulus acquired his information, one imagines, in some such way as this: the *lucumo* of Tarquinia, one day toward the middle of the eighth century B.C., was pleased to grant an audience to a delegation from Latium who had crossed the Tiber to seek his advice. The Latins wished to found a new settlement, their spokesman told the *lucumo,* who sat before them like a god enthroned; and they had come to learn the proper way to found it.

The place where the Latin people were at present settled, the delegation explained, was not, for many reasons, altogether satisfactory; yet they had been living there long enough to have buried their fathers in the earth. How, then, could they settle elsewhere without incurring the wrath of their ancestors?

A difficult problem, the *lucumo* admitted. His Tarquinia, he had learned in early childhood, had been founded according to the ruling of Tages, and the city had prospered beyond all expectations. Was it wise to divulge the sacred rites to an alien people? He must first consult his *haruspex,* he decided, and possibly the chief men of nearby Etruscan cities. But that thought he at once discarded, for he, like his peers, was strongly individualistic and did not care to listen to ideas that might clash with his own. And since his city was the oldest and the strongest in Etruria, and his *haruspex* the wisest as well as the most respected, the decision must be theirs alone.

"Where do you wish to re-settle?" the *lucumo* of Tarquinia inquired gravely.

The delegation told him that their proposed site was a hill near the Tiber; the site had been revealed to their leader Romulus by a flight of twelve vultures overhead. It was an advantageous situation, the spokesman added, for it would give them access to the Tyrrhenian Sea. The *lucumo* consulted his *haruspex,* and together they came to their decision to reveal the sacred founding rites to Romulus.

However it came about, on April 21, 753 B.C. one of the most important events in the history of the world occurred; Rome was founded. For Etruria, though, on that same day were sown the seeds of her ultimate downfall.

The Romans, the Greeks, and the Etruscans believed that the prospective site of a city was revealed to them by a supernatural power, acting through a human being. For the Romans, the instrument was Romulus; for the Greeks, a Messenian; and for the Etruscans, Tages. Tages sprang from the earth. The Messenian, directed by a dream, dug in the earth where he found a "yew tree . . . near a myrtle," and discovered an urn upon whose "leaves of tin" were engraved the founding rites to be followed. Once founded, a city became the sanctuary for its people, its boundaries guarded, not by its warriors, but by its sacred fire and its ancestral gods.

When the *haruspices* from Tarquinia had chosen the proper spot on the Palatine Hill, a fire of brushwood was lighted, and each man who had come with Romulus to the new site leaped over the fire, to purify himself of all clinging evil.

The *haruspices* then commanded Romulus to dig a round hole, or trench, in the place where he wished to locate the center of his city. This trench, or *mundus*, was to be the channel through which the deified dead, when transferred to their new home, and the dead who would later be buried in the new site, might visit the upper world on the specified three days of the year. And so in the trench each man reverently placed a clod of the earth he had brought with him for his express purpose. (Plutarch says *first fruits*. Earth is more likely, since this would symbolize the transfer of the buried ancestor to his new home.)

The next rite Romulus had to perform was to set the boundary line of his new city. He yoked a white bull and a white cow to a bronze plowshare. With his head veiled and wearing sacred garments, probably similar to those worn by an Etruscan *haruspex*, Romulus drove a deep furrow around the *mundus*, following his sacred line. Upon or over this line no man could step without angering the gods. This was the line Roman tradition says Remus stepped over, and paid with his life for his fault.

Men had followed closely after Romulus to watch the clods as they were turned up. Any clod or piece of earth that fell outward, they reversed. Since there had to be ways of entering and leaving the city without either stepping on the boundary line or overstepping it, Romulus had lifted his plow where gates were to be and had carried it over the intervening space.

A city laid out according to this Etruscan ritual may have been circular, perhaps like the recently discovered Teotihuacán, northeast of Mexico City. But in Teotihuacán the Avenue of the Dead ran straight through the center with its "pyramids and temples, markets and assembly plazas, beyond lay homes and farm lands. . . ."

The excavated cities of Etruria show straight streets running at right angles to one another. Marzobotta near Bologna, Spina founded by the Etruscans, and part of early Pompeii have straight streets. The streets of Etruscan Vetulonia, on the other hand, wind about and cross one another as irregularly as those of Fiesole today.

Whether circular or quadrilateral, a city laid out according to what is believed to be the divine will gives to its citizens a feeling of "belonging" to an established place where they have a god-given right to be and for which they will fight to the death. If its boundaries are violated, however, and its sacred fire either defiled or destroyed, then retribution follows. It may be that only the defiler pays with his life as Remus did; it may be that the gods have forsaken their people and nothing remains that is worth the fight.

Ritually established in their new cities, the Etruscans built a society that rested upon the authority of the *lucumo,* who had in his keeping the sacred fire of the city, open to all citizens but to no outsiders.

Pallotino feels that the title *lucumo* refers to the Etruscan kings of the archaic period, when each city-state was ruled by a chief, or *lucumo.* An aristocratic king or ruler, the *lucumo* was also a priest, trained from boyhood to interpret to his people the mystical utterance of Tages, their first religious teacher and law-giver.

In this connection it is interesting to recall that the Greek philosopher, Pythagoras, who in the sixth century B.C. established a religious brotherhood in southern Italy, is often called a *lucumo.* The name appeared again in the eighteenth century when some enthusiastic Italians formed an Etruscan Academy and called their president *lucumo,* but by this time the title had obviously retained only its secular meaning, since the Etruscan Academy was not a religious organization.

Etruria was, of course, a monarchy, composed of city-states, each governed by its *lucumo.* Livy describes Tolumnius, the *lucumo* of Veii, galloping ahead of his warriors, "shining far over the field of battle through the unique splendour of his royal raiment." To the *lucumo* belonged all the trappings of ancient royalty: the crown of gold, the purple-embroidered robe, the state throne, the gold ring of office, and the *fasces,* the bundle of rods with its double-bladed axe.

Four times a year—at each phase of the moon—the *lucumo* showed himself in public. His face painted vermilion, his person robed in a cloak embroidered with stars, the eagle-topped scepter in his hand, the *lucumo* rode forth in a chariot drawn by white horses. In a solemn ceremony the *lucumo* performed the sacrifices for his people, and by virtue of the sanctity within him, made known what the future held in store.

We are told that the *lucumones* fought on horseback or from chariots—the Etruscans are said to have introduced the chariot into Italy—and that at first all military equipment was pre-Hellenic, double-bladed axes and short, curved swords with triangular blades. Contact with Greece gradually changed the character of the earlier equipment, though Etruscan armor continued to be made of bronze. Each *lucumo* raised his own army, by calling upon his fellow-patricians to gather their serfs and slaves together and follow him into battle. Years had to pass before anything even remotely like a national army would come into existence. Then it was too late.

Along with the remarkable sophistication of the ritual observance controlling the community organization of the Etruscans goes, of course, a strangely simple and primitive life. Hunting and fishing, so widely illustrated in the paintings, were not really sports; they kept the city alive. Men and boys of all classes engaged in this necessary occupation. A pillar in one of the tombs at Cerveteri shows a huntsman's bag, the rudder of a boat, and a goose.

In the Tomb of Hunting and Fishing at Tarquinia, which consists of two rooms with a connecting door, a hunting scene is painted on the pediment over the door. The colors are still vivid, reds and greens predominating. From a background of trees and bushes huntsmen emerge returning from the chase. Two young men on horseback are preceded by a slave who is urging on the dogs. Under a bush crouches a frightened hare. One of the dogs has spied the small creature, and seems about to spring.

Behind the horsemen come more slaves, two carrying game suspended from a pole, another the knobbed sticks the Greeks and Romans used in flushing out hares. Both ends of the pediment are filled with the trees and shrubs of an Etruscan landscape.

The famous Certosa *situla,* a bronze bucket in the Civic Museum of Bologna, also shows a hunting party. Some carry a deer slung from a pole; others drag a dead boar; excited dogs leap around the hunters. Aelian, in his *History of Animals,* says that Etruscan hunters used flute-players to charm animals into their traps. The music floats up into the hills and down into the valleys and finds its way into the hidden dens. Charmed by the sound, the animals leave their dens and even their young and hasten toward the music. Unaware of the traps, they fall into them and are caught. A tomb painting shows horses, beaters, and dogs driving a boar into the nets.

The *situla* shows farmers with their oxen. His oxen plodding along in front of him, a weary farmer comes down a rocky hillside, his plow balanced on his shoulder. Miniature terra-cottas in the Gregorian Museum and also in the Villa Giulia complete the picture with their crude, but life-like representations of farmers and oxen.

Military processions are shown on the *situla*. One is being watched by two friends who listen to the music while they drink their wine. Perhaps they wonder who is being honored with a military funeral, for both cavalry and infantry parade by with lances dipped. Perhaps when the warrior reaches his final resting-place, he will see his weapons, both defensive and offensive, already painted on the wall; his armor, too, conveniently to hand when he needs it in the new life he is to lead.

The horses in the other military procession are magnificent, prancing creatures. In the tomb paintings the horses are strangely represented by the convention of red bodies, white tails, and blue hoofs. So Dennis says he saw them in an early painting in the cemetery of Tarquinia, the so-called Tomb of the Barons. Behind the horsemen on the *situla* march groups of foot soldiers; their shields show great variety, a round shield here, there an oval one, and there one that is rectangular. Their helmets are equally varied. Clearly no uniformity has yet been achieved.

Archaeology has now confirmed the tradition that Tarquinia is the oldest of the scattered Etruscan cities, and that she was generally regarded as the metropolis. From Tarquinia her warriors set forth to conquer the country. Until the close of her history, which begins in the ninth century B.C., or even earlier, she remained the most powerful and the most respected of the central confederation of the twelve cities, sometimes referred to as the Union of the Rasenna. She held her own during the next two centuries, industrially and commercially. Intellectual and artistic contacts with the East and with Greece, through overseas trade, helped to mold the fresh Etruscan mind in Tarquinia, Chiusi, Veii, and wherever else that contacts were made.

If we could transport ourselves to seventh-century Tarquinia and stroll through her streets, we could understand why her people thought themselves safe from invasion. Built on a hill of volcanic rock that rises high and steep and encircled by strong walls, the city should be able to repel any attack.

Life within would seem busy and secure. In the center would lie the *mundus,* and from it would run streets, lined on either side by houses with peaked roofs. Naked children would play on the pavement or leap across the street on high stepping-stones; oxen and carts would rumble past, their drivers casting an occasional glance across the wooded valley to the opposite hill where the homes of the dead rose, easy of access for the living.

Our ears would be beset by strange speech, unlike anything we had ever heard, impossible to understand or even to classify. We might try a word or two, in languages we knew, be met with smiles and head-shakings, and turn away, puzzled, and slightly shamed, since all our erudition had availed us nothing.

If we crossed the Tiber, recently bridged, we should see, instead of mansions, small round huts built on the hills which dip their feet in a great swamp, destined in later days to become the famous Roman Forum. Excavations have now revealed those early habitations of the City of the She-Wolf; and the contrast between the settlement there and the Etruscan cities of the same period startles the onlooker into fresh admiration of the changes we know the three Etruscan kings gradually brought about during their occupation of Rome (716 B.C.–509 B.C.).

Romulus and his group of hardy adventurers had no women among them. Fearful of leaving no offspring to succeed them, they decided to hold a festival and invite the neighbors to inspect their new city. All the nearby peoples flocked in, bringing with them their wives and children. Among the guests were the Sabines. The Romans were most hospitable—they had announced a show—and when the frolic was at its height and the watch over the women was relaxed, the young Romans rushed in and abducted all the virgins they could lay hands on, by tradition more than six hundred.

Time passed; the City of the She-Wolf grew strong; the Elders formed themselves into a body that derived its power from the worship of their ancestors. Romulus, eager to increase his own power as the chief of state, inevitably came into conflict with the Senate, as the new body came to be called, since they were the *Senes,* the old ones. To free himself, Romulus sought the favor of the lower classes, captives and stragglers whose cause he championed. One day Romulus disappeared in a clap of thunder, caught up to the skies, the Senate piously explained when they instituted appropriate rites in his honor.

Meanwhile across the Tiber the Etruscans went their prosperous way, less concerned with the growing pains of Rome than with the steady arrival on their shores of Greek immigrants who, from the seventh century on, braved the dangers of the Adriatic Sea to round the toe of Italy, venture into Tyrrhenian waters that were infested with pirates, and gain access to the new Western cities whose repute had spread far.

One day a notable group came from wealthy Corinth, led by a certain Demaratus who had rebelled against a law that forbade him to buy land. With Demaratus came his sympathizers, many of them skilled in the arts. The group settled in Tarquinia. There Demaratus married a patrician lady who gave him two sons. The elder he called, oddly enough, Lucumo, the younger he called by the good Etruscan name, Aruns.

Other strangers came, too, and were not repulsed. They scattered among the cities: artisans to seek a better livelihood, traders to exploit the riches they had heard sailors boast of; and some sources tell us, painters and sculptors also came. Soon Etruria was the strongest economic power in Italy.

The enormous slag-heaps of northern Etruria and the great quantity of the glossy black earthenware the Italians call *bucchero* that have been found in Britain show that the Etruscans soon became a prosperous commercial people. The copper and iron they mined in the north, near Populonia, provided enough purchasing power to enable them to import all the gold and silver their craftsmen needed. To protect their trade, they required sea power strong enough to hold their own against the surrounding peoples, all intent on gaining control over the raw materials, especially the rich mine deposits of Spain, Sardinia, and Italy. Greek literature abounds with references to the greed and cruelty of those Tyrrhenian pirates whom we now call Etruscans. One particularly gruesome tale recounts the custom of lashing together a dead prisoner and a live one and casting both into the sea.

Gradually the Etruscan fleet, probably composed of ships belonging to the coastal cities, completely dominated the Tyrrhenian Sea, and colonizing of the regions south of Rome, the rich plains of Campania, began. Inland, the city of Veii, closer to Rome than Tarquinia was, and grown wealthy from the proceeds of her salt-works at the mouth of the Tiber, became involved with Ancus Marcius, the third king of Rome after Romulus, in a struggle over her continued possession of the salt-works. The struggle was not new; according to tradition Romulus himself had disputed Veii's right to own property at the mouth of the Tiber, and to protect herself Veii had established there an Etruscan settlement, called the Seven Villages.

The dispute was still raging when, in the seventh century B.C., Lucumo, the elder son of Demaratus, the Greek refugee from Corinth who had settled in Tarquinia, came with his wife, Tanaquil, to Rome. Here Lucumo quickly became known as Lucius Tarquinius, a wealthy Etruscan nobleman, interested in the future of the infant City of the She-Wolf.

XIII

The First Etruscan King of Rome

(616 B.C.—578 B.C.)

The seventh century B.C. had already passed its mid-mark when one day peasants breaking stones on the summit of the Janiculum Hill saw laboring up the far side of the hill a pair of noble black stallions, whose like the peasants had never seen before. Shading their eyes against the glare of the westering sun, the workmen now saw that the stallions were harnessed to a leather-hooded traveling carriage, its bronze sides splashed with mud.

The carriage braked to a stop alongside the men. Its richly-dressed occupants, obviously even to peasant eyes a young nobleman and his lady, bent forward in their seats to gaze eagerly down into the valley below. Then they turned and smiled radiantly at each other. The young nobleman, still smiling, rose and looked back down the hill. The peasants, open-mouthed, looked too. Several heavily-loaded wagons were toiling up. The nobleman waved a beckoning hand.

At that instant a wondrous thing happened. An eagle swooped down from the sky, snatched off the nobleman's tall pointed cap, and winged swiftly upward, carrying its prize. Twice the great bird circled high overhead, swooped down again, and replaced the tall cap. Such, in essence, with a few embellishments, is Livy's account of the arrival of Lucumo, the son of a foreign-born father and an Etruscan mother, on the rocky summit of the Janiculum Hill.

It was a restless time for young Etruscan men, for Etruria was strengthening her hold on Italy by founding new cities and pushing her commerce into all quarters of the Mediterranean world. Doubtless Lucumo was also restless, but Livy does not mention this as a reason for his coming to Rome. Tanaquil's marriage, he observes, was frowned upon by aristocratic Tarquinia, and this slight neither Lucumo nor his high-spirited and ambitious Tanaquil would brook. And so Lucumo listened when Tanaquil urged him to cross the Tiber and seek his fortune in Rome.

When the eagle replaced Lucumo's cap, Tanaquil knew she had been right; to her the eagle's action was a mark of divine favor, and she hastened to interpret the omen to her husband. She advised him to prepare for the high destiny that awaited him in Rome by changing his name to its Latin equivalent, Lucius. Soon, under his new name, Lucumo arrived in Rome and eventually introduced himself to King Ancus Marcius as Lucius Tarquinius, or, according to one tradition, as Lucius Sextus Tarquinius. Later history knows the young foreigner as Tarquin the Elder.

Tanaquil's powers of divination and interpretation never deserted her throughout her long life in her adopted city. Tradition credits her with having elevated to the throne not only her husband, but also his successor, Servius Tullius. Yet, though Livy knew of Tanaquil, archaeology knew nothing about her until 1832. In that year a *Camera del Morte,* or Dead Man's Chamber, was discovered in Tarquinia. Only about eight feet square, a little over six feet high in the center and about five on the sides, the Chamber was the smallest tomb that had so far been unearthed.

Still visible on a side wall, at the time of the tomb's discovery, was a fairly well-preserved painting that has been detached and is now in the Gregorian Museum. The painting shows the body of an elderly man lying on his funeral couch. Over him a young girl bends, her hand about to draw his hood over his eyes. She wears a long, close-fitting robe; her braided hair falls, Etruscan fashion, over her shoulders; and her feet are shod in long, sharp-toed shoes.

Written in Etruscan characters above the girl's head is a name, Thanueil. Dennis suggests that a slight change in the letters would make Thanchavil, the Etruscan form of Tanaquil. Over the body of the elderly man the name Thanorseia is written, also in Etruscan characters, and Dennis would like to think that this is the name of Tanaquil's father.

In the same tomb a sarcophagus was also found and taken to the Gregorian Museum. The inscription on its architrave reads, *Eca Suthi Thanchvilus Masnial,* which Dennis thinks may mean "here is the tomb of Tanaquil."

If Dennis has correctly identified Tanaquil and her father, perhaps his death rather than the stigma Livy says she suffered because of her marriage to the son of a foreigner may have led her to urge Lucumo to quit Tarquinia for Rome. There she may have hoped to find people less clannish.

Livy does not mention Tanaquil's appearance; instead he stresses what he considers the dominant trait of her character, her ambition. Later writers also refer to this, and some even go so far as to conjecture that her ambition may have been instrumental in causing the ultimate downfall of the Tarquin dynasty. Festus, an historian and antiquarian of the fourth century A.D., adds a picturesque touch to Tanaquil's reputation; he asserts that she wore as an amulet, a magic belt, or girdle. In Greek mythology, the goddess Aphrodite also wore a magic girdle. Perhaps Festus means us to think of Tanaquil as possessing irresistible beauty.

Etruscan women, if we judge them by some of the portraits in our museums, especially that of the lady Velca, were as handsome as their Tuscan descendants of today. And so we may not wrong the lady Tanaquil if we ascribe to her a face as beautiful as that of Velca in the Orcus Tomb in Tarquinia.

To Lucius and Tanaquil, coming from the older and better-ordered Etruria, with its walled cities and cobbled roads, its brightly-painted temples and well-built houses, Rome surely appeared mean and uncouth, with nothing to predict its future majesty. The Forum was still a swamp; cemeteries lay just beyond reach of its mud; streets were unpaved, even those leading up to the modest palace on the Palatine Hill, where Lucius, after he had established Tanaquil and himself in humbler quarters, came to make himself known.

Affable, generous, and wealthy, tradition tells us, Lucius could have had no difficulty in housing himself in seventh-century Rome. Probably among his retinue were men skilled in building houses, round, square, or rectangular. Of details such as these we know nothing. Tradition has King Ancus Marcius extending an invitation to Lucius and Tanaquil to leave their quarters and make his palace their permanent home.

Ancus Marcius, the son of a Sabine mother and a Latin father, had become in 740 B.C. the third king of Rome after Romulus. Liberal and democratic, a contrast to his predecessor, he had soon earned the title of Father of the Plebs. Before he ascended the throne, he had been active in promoting Mediterranean trade; afterward, when the Latins rose against him, thinking he would set peace above war, he fought and conquered them. The inhabitants of the cities he captured he transferred to Rome, then razed their cities to the ground. In this ruthless way the Aventine Hill was populated. The Roman custom of uprooting helpless peoples and colonizing them elsewhere contributed greatly to the later disruption and conquest of one Etruscan city after the other.

Livy credits Ancus Marcius with forethought in building the first bridge over the Tiber, the famous Pons Sublicius, that rested on wooden piles driven deep into the river bed and without metal clamps or supports. The king had had the bridge built to connect the Janiculum Hill, which he had annexed and fortified, with the rest of the city. To make the city doubly secure against invasion, he had had the bridge constructed in such a way that it could be taken to pieces and removed. Plutarch ridicules the belief, current in his day, that the priests, or Pontifices, who were in charge of the sacrifices on the bridge, were called bridge-makers because among their duties was that of keeping the bridge in good condition.

King Ancus soon realized that the uprooted peoples in the city caused over-crowding and in time brought about a "population-explosion" that led men of base instincts to take to a life of crime as more exciting and more advantageous than a sober life of unremitting toil. To protect honest citizens against these criminals, Ancus built in the center of the city a prison that seems always to have been kept full, even over-crowded.

Ancus Marcius was gratified when the young Etruscan nobleman, whom he knew as Lucius Tarquinius, came with his aristocratic wife Tanaquil to his palace to live, because he had two young sons and he had been troubled about having them educated as became young Roman princes. When he observed that Lucius was an educated man, the king entrusted his sons to his care. As time passed, Lucius gained a higher position than that of royal tutor; he became the aging king's most trusted adviser. How Tanaquil passed her days in the palace in unknown; though we do know that she brought up there her own two children, a daughter and a son.

It was the custom in early Rome for a king to choose his successor and present him to the people for acceptance or rejection. This choice Lucius, and probably Tanaquil, kept urging Ancus Marcius to make. On the appointed day, which the king had finally agreed to, Lucius sent the young princes off on a long hunting expedition. Then he appeared before the assembled people to present his own qualifications for the throne. Livy has preserved what purports to be his speech. In it Lucius states boldly that the people may as well elect him, since for many years he has been their ruler, not in name, but in reality.

The people voted to accept Lucius Tarquinius, the courteous nobleman whom many had come to know and to approve of. And so in 616 B.C. Lucumo, the son of Demaratus of Corinth, became the first Etruscan king of Rome. Livy tells us that Tarquin's inauguration was celebrated in the Etruscan fashion, a fashion which prevailed until the exasperated Roman people, a hundred years later, put an end to the Etruscan monarchy.

The young princes returned to find their royal father dead, their erstwhile tutor on the throne, and, by their father's will, their legal guardian. Unable, for the time being, to organize a movement against the Etruscan who, from their point of view, had usurped the throne, they withdrew from Rome.

Early in his reign, Tarquin realized that, to offset the liberal and democratic tendency Ancus Marcius had fostered, he needed fresh support, especially in the Senate. To gain this, he selected a hundred men from non-patrician families and elevated them to the Senate. He soon bound them to his regime by conferring favors upon them, high political offices and business opportunities, such as managing the revenues from the Etruscan salt-works at the mouth of the Tiber.

The key to prosperity, Tarquin also realized, lay in trade with the Greek colonies in southern Italy, but Latin tribes blocked the land route and had to be reckoned with. Meanwhile he set on foot various grandiose projects, among them a great Circus for the performance of games. These projects cost money. To refill his depleted treasury, Tarquin waged a successful war with the Latins. Upon his return he entertained the populace with a lavish display of games, which greatly pleased them. About this time he began to build a wall around the city. An attack by the Sabines, though indecisive, made him aware of the weakness of his cavalry, who had never learned to dismount and fight on foot. Nor did Tarquin urge them to change, since this was the Etruscan fashion. Instead, he doubled their number.

Tarquin had intended to change the organization of the cavalry, but this, a seer told him in no uncertain terms, would be impossible until the usual omens could be drawn from observing the flight of birds. The incredulous Tarquin declared that he would believe in the seer's ability to interpret omens only if he would consent to accomplish what he himself had in mind. The seer consented. Tarquin then placed a whetstone before him and ordered him to cleave it with a razor. The seer did so. Ever afterward, Livy states, no innovation in Rome was undertaken if the birds signified their disapproval, as they must have, for at that time no reorganization seems to have taken place.

In spite of the increase in his fighting forces, Tarquin might have lost in the final clash with the Sabines, had he not devised a clever stratagem. The Sabines had left their boats anchored down stream in the Anio River and had crossed a bridge into Roman territory. Tarquin ordered his men to gather wood, set it ablaze, and throw it into the river. Luck was with him; a breeze sprang up and carried the blazing wood against the piers of the bridge where the Sabines had left their boats. Frantic, the enemy tried to escape by swimming back across the river. Their floating shields told of their defeat long before the official news arrived.

The Sabines sued for peace. One small city, Collatia, continued the struggle. When it could no longer hold out, Tarquin accepted its surrender, sent in a strong garrison to keep its unruly inhabitants in order, and appointed Egerius, his nephew from Tarquinia, commander. Elated by his success, Tarquin next attacked and destroyed the Latin stronghold at Alba Longa. Never rebuilt, today its site is familiar to many, because the Pope's summer residence, Castel Gandolfo, is near by.

Tarquin now ordered the Senate to vote him a triumph. The new Senators he had appointed over-ruled all objections and, for the first time in history, Livy declares, a victorious king, magnificently dressed, rode in his war-chariot through the streets of Etruscan Rome.

Later, in the days of the Roman Empire, a triumphal procession began at the city gates, progressed through cheering crowds to the Sacred Way and the Forum, and ended when the Emperor dismounted from his chariot at the foot of the high steps leading to the temple of Jupiter on the Capitoline Hill, the temple that some say Tarquin hinself began to build not to the Roman Jupiter but to the Etruscan Tinia. In Tarquin's day a triumph may not have extended so far. Perhaps the chariot he rode in resembled the bronze Etruscan war-chariot in the Metropolitan Museum in New York. With four spirited white horses attached to such a chariot as this, on which its painted scenes and some of its original gold wash are still visible, Tarquin would have made a lasting impression on his subjects, especially if he had had his face painted red, as Etruscan ritual demanded of a *lucumo.*

A small gilded silver bowl from the Bernardini Tomb near Palestrina shows a bare-headed warrior, but Tarquin, one imagines, was resplendent in a crested helmet like that worn by a warrior on a tomb from Vetulonia; his head is protected by a close-fitting helmet topped by a tall crest with a long, pointed tail that touches the center of the round shield on his left arm. Aloft in his right hand, the warrior holds his doubled-bladed battle axe.

If Tarquin's successful war with Veii, the fifth in the struggle for possession of the salt-works, took place before he celebrated his triumph, he may have used the occasion to introduce to Rome the Etruscan symbols of royalty, traditionally adopted about this time: the gold crown, the ivory chair, the purple robe, and the eagle-headed scepter. Some think, however, that the Etruscans presented these symbols to Tarquin when he seized the throne. If this view can be depended upon, the twelve lictors Livy mentions may have walked before his chariot, one from each of the twelve Etruscan cities which formed themselves, either in Tarquin's day or later, into the Union of the Rasenna.

These twelve lictors, whether they were an Etruscan innovation or not, were official bodyguards. Each man carried on his left shoulder a bundle of slender rods, in early days made of elm, later of birch, tied together with a red thong. From each bundle a double-bladed axe protruded. Thus equipped, the lictors were prepared to take instant action.

Tradition ascribes to Tarquin an innovation that gradually brought about a far-reaching change in the mercantile life of

Rome. He drained off the water of the marshes by a series of ditches, all sloping toward the Tiber, and on the reclaimed land provided an opportunity for a civic center, which afterward grew into the great Roman Forum. As trade increased, the barter system gave way and lumps of copper were used as a medium of exchange.

But lumps of copper were heavy and clumsy, and when, early in the sixth century, business men learned that in southern Italy, where Greek colonies were flourishing, small easily handled copper coins were in use, Tarquin established a coinage system in Rome. The spur to business activity and the consequent increase in revenue almost compensated him for the trouble the Greek colonies were causing. Soon he would have to interfere with their seizure of Etruscan ports that afforded access to the rich mine fields of Corsica and Sardinia.

Meanwhile, as tradition preserves the story, an old woman appeared one day at the palace and demanded audience of the King. She said she had come from Cumae in southern Italy to sell him twelve books that were important to the future of Rome. The price she asked was exorbitant, and Tarquin curtly dismissed her. Later, the old woman reappeared with nine books—she said she had destroyed three—and asked the same price as before. Tarquin again dismissed her. But when he heard that she had destroyed three more and that she was threatening to sell the other six to his enemies, he succumbed and bought them at the original price.

A variant tradition states that Tarquin resisted until only three books survived. These he bought at the price asked for twelve. Whatever the number of these oracular books (the famous Sibylline books) that passed into the ownership of Rome, they were put in a secure place and guards posted over them. In crises, these books were always consulted. The legend of the Sibylline books (whether bought by Tarquin or by a successor) is sometimes interpreted to mean that the Etruscan alphabet may have come from Cumae, and not from the East. The discovery in Cumae of a large drinking cup, a *scyphus*, with partial sentences composed of words separated by dots similar to those found in other Etruscan inscriptions partially supports this theory.

In the royal household lived a young slave-boy of unknown birth, Servius Tullius. A generally accepted Roman tradition runs that one day Tanaquil came upon the boy sound asleep. About to awaken him, she was startled to see a flame hovering above his head. Tarquin, hastily summoned, also saw the flame. The frightened King and Queen awakened the boy. When he opened his eyes, the flame disappeared. Convinced of the boy's high destiny, Tanaquil persuaded her husband to let her supervise his education. Then when the proper time came, she had him betrothed to her daughter.

According to the confused chronology of the period, Servius Tullius was a grown man and a favored member of the royal family when the self-exiled sons of Ancus Marcius reappeared in Rome, apparently without the knowledge of Tarquin or Tanaquil.

Tarquin seems to have been accustomed to receiving in person all who had complaints. One day while he was seated upon his throne, judging cases, two quarreling herdsmen shouldered their way into the palace. Each had his axe with him. One began to present his case. Tarquin leaned forward to hear him; instantly the other buried his axe in the King's head. In the uproar that followed, the herdsmen escaped from the palace and were lost in the crowd of waiting petitioners.

The resourceful Tanaquil at once took charge. She had reached her husband's side only a few seconds before he died. Since he had no son to succeed him—Tarquin's only son had been killed in battle—Tanaquil ordered the palace closed and guarded. Then she urged Servius Tullius to mount the throne; she herself would speak to the crowd outside. Leaving her protégé seated upon the throne, she hurried upstairs, flung open a window, announced that the King was ill, and that meanwhile all were to obey Servius Tullius. A few days later Tanaquil announced the King's death.

Livy suggests that the sons of Ancus Marcius had paid the

herdsmen to murder Tarquin, also that they started a rumor in the city that brought an unusually large crowd to mill about outside the palace and so provide the assassins with the cover for their escape.

According to Roman chronology, which begins with the founding of Rome, Tarquin the Elder, the first Etruscan king, was murdered in one hundred and seventy-six; according to our chronology it was the year five hundred and seventy-eight before Christ.

The Emperor Augustus claimed that he found Rome a city built of brick, but that he left it a city built of marble. Tarquin the Elder, despite the legendary character of his rule, might well have claimed that he found Ruma a collection of huts in a swamp, but that he left Rome a small thriving settlement through which men could walk, dry-shod.

XIV

The Fire-Begotten King

(578 B.C. — 534 B.C.)

Servius Tullius steps out upon the stage of history with shreds of fancy and of fact clinging to the name we know him by. The oldest legend associated with him goes back to the days before his birth; it is also the oldest, Charles Leland thinks, in the long list of supernatural births.

The legend asserts that the child over whose head Tarquin and Tanaquil saw flames hovering was begotten by the sacred hearth-fire in the palace, and that his mother was Ocresia, the woman Mayani has identified from the inscription on the Tarchon mirror. According to Mayani, Ocresia is a well-known Etruscan name.

All versions of Ocresia's strange story connect her with Corniculum, a town that King Tarquin had captured in one of his numerous military expeditions. After slaughtering the king of Corniculum and other leading men, Tarquin left the town to be destroyed and went back to Rome, taking with him the women and children. Among the women was the king's daughter, Ocresia. At this point in the story there is discussion as to whether the captive girl was a virgin, or whether she was pregnant.

According to a third version, Ocresia was not a captive princess from Corniculum, but a slave from Alba Longa. The king of Alba Longa had ordered his daughter to go to the palace in Rome to serve the monarch's pleasure.

Whoever Ocresia was, at the palace she was required to serve Tarquin and Tanaquil at the table. One day she was sent to the hearth to offer food to the domestic gods. She placed the food on the blazing logs and instantly a *phallus* sprang toward her from the flames. Legend adds that Tanaquil interpreted the meaning of the apparition as a "revelation by the lar, or genius, of the royal family, predicting an extraordinary birth in the house."

Tarquin accepted his Queen's interpretation and commanded Ocresia to dress in bridal garments and sit near the hearth, not, like Cinderella, in the ashes, because that would mean quenching the fire. Seated in the heat of the fire, Ocresia conceived and when her time came, she bore a son and she called him Servius Tullius. And once while the boy was sleeping, his hair "appeared like fire." It is worth noting that all versions of the birth story mention the boy's "flame-like hair."

The boy was named Servius Tullius. One wishes he had been called Rufus, for then the story of his fiery, or flame-like, hair would be easily accounted for: he was a redhead. But the boy's name was Servius, given him, it has been suggested, because of its similarity to *servus*, the Latin word for slave.

Until recently Servius Tullius has been regarded as a patriotic Roman who restored the democratic ideals of Ancus Marcius. This view was not seriously challenged until a bronze tablet was found in Lyon on which was recorded a speech of the Emperor Claudius (the supposed author of the lost Etruscan history) in which he states that Servius Tullius was only another name for the Etruscan Mastarna.

Two recent archaeological discoveries have added to this identification: one is a wall-painting from Vulci, the other a fragment of a *bucchero* vase (black glazed pottery) from Veii. The painting, a fresco of the fourth century B.C. or possibly later, was found on the wall of a tomb-chamber in Vulci. Though almost unknown to classical literature, ancient Vulci was at that time one of the wealthiest of the many luxury-loving cities of Etruria, with cemeteries that contained some twenty thousand graves. Discovered in the nineteenth century while scientific archaeology was still in its infancy, the rich contents of these graves were ruthlessly plundered. Fortunately, most, if not all of the plunder eventually reached the Villa Giulia, the Louvre, and the British Museum.

The fresco, which Pallotino thinks belongs to the end of the second or the beginning of the first century B.C., shows a battle between the Etruscans and the Romans; along the margin of the fresco the names of the combatants appear, written in Etruscan characters. One is Macstrna, the Mastarna of literary tradition, who is known to have participated in the revolt of Vulci against Tarquin's Rome. Two brothers, Aulus and Caelius Vibenna, led the revolt. In the fresco, the brothers and Mastarna are fighting desperately against the Romans. Caelius is already down, and Mastarna is trying in vain to protect him. One of the Romans is also down; written above him is Cneve Tarchumies Rumach, the name of a warrior of the Tarquin family. From this scene may have come the variant tradition that Servius Tullius (Mastarna) killed his predecessor.

The other recent discovery which has helped to identify Mastarna as an Etruscan is the fragment of the *bucchero* vase from Veii, found in the sanctuary of Apollo, where it was obviously placed as a thank-offering to the god. Its inscription "Avile Vipiinnas dedicated me," is self-revealing. Avile is Aulus, the brother who, with the help of Mastarna, escaped alive from the conflict. He has shown his gratitude by dedicating a vase to Apollo.

Classical tradition holds that Caelius Vibenna, assisted by his brother and Mastarna, seized Rome and ruled the city until, under mysterious circumstances, Caelius disappeared. Mastarna succeeded him as Servius Tullius. The Emperor Augustus was evidently aware of this tradition, which keeps Rome under Etruscan control.

Dionysius says that the revolt against Tarquin's Rome occurred in the first year of Servius Tullius' reign. Tarquinia, Veii, and Cerveteri supported Vulci in a war that lasted twenty years and ended in the complete subjugation of the Confederation of the Twelve Cities, a mysterious organization sometimes called the Union of the Rasenna but of which little is known that is not the subject of controversy.

It is useless to try to reconcile these diverse traditions about the birth and identity of Servius Tullius. Some authorities accept the tradition that Mastarna was a rebel who killed Tarquin in battle and, by right of conquest, ascended the throne. As the second Etruscan king of Rome, he became identified with Servius Tullius. This point of view many scholars now accept.

Livy states that Servius Tullius was the first king of Rome to rule without having been elected by the people. Notwithstanding this, the new king's first reform was to give lands to the lower classes, not in the city itself, but in territory taken from conquered peoples. For families who had always cultivated the fields of others, this was an exciting innovation and increased the king's popularity, not, however, with the patricians who saw their way of life threatened.

The other reforms usually attributed to King Servius (especially the census and the reorganization of the army on a property basis) are disputed. Those who deny him the census insist that the first official count of Roman citizens was really taken in 443 B.C., long after the fall of the Etruscan monarchy in Italy. Livy, who accepts the tradition of the earlier census, declares that the fear and the hostility of the peasants was such that they hid their horses in the woods and barricaded themselves in their houses.

To count the free inhabitants of the city, King Servius is said to have assembled all men, patricians and plebeians, in the place that afterward became the Campus Martius. Eighty thousand men responded when their names were called. Livy states that this count was held in 577 B.C., the second year of the new king's reign.

De Coulanges tells us that the king then "walked around this mixed assembly, driving victims before him, and singing solemn hymns. The ceremony finished, all alike found themselves citizens." The victims on this occasion may have been a pig, a sheep, and a bull, because similar animals were sacrificed when King Servius finally built his new army and assembled them in the Campus Martius to be ritually purified.

King Servius was now able to institute a tax system. This brought an even greater outcry, from the patricians most of all; he also required of all unmarried women an annual sum for the upkeep of a specified number of soldiers, a law that went into effect when he later reformed the army. Before or afterward he devalued the copper *as* (the basis Tarquin had set for the coinage system he introduced into Rome) by reducing its weight.

Convinced that many plebeians were as financially able as the patricians to equip themselves for war and also able to bear part of the costs of maintaining a sound government, King Servius used the taxes to build an infantry composed entirely of plebeians who would be equipped and maintained by the state. This revolutionary act pleased the commons. But it terrified the patricians; they foresaw atrocities at the hands of rough, untrained soldiery who might at any moment take it into their heads to turn their newly acquired weapons upon their betters.

The new army was assembled in the Campus Martius. The method of sacrifice may have been that shown on two sepulchral urns from Etruria. On one urn a priest pours a libation over the head of a sacrificial animal. The other urn shows more detail. Two men hold an animal by a chain; a third pours a libation over the animal's head; then a fourth strikes him down with an axe.

From this time on, all free men who owned property were members of the army; the poor alone were excluded. A distinction continued to be made, not by caste, but by wealth, the first class— Servius divided the people into five classes—being composed of those who were able to equip themselves with full armor, or at least with shield, helmet, and sword. The cavalry remained a separate body, but a certain number of wealthy plebeians now entered the patrician ranks. These innovations increased the importance of the plebeians and made them devoted followers of the king.

Excavations in the Roman Forum have shown that in 575 B.C., three years after Servius Tullius became king, Rome's first pavement was laid down. The pavement is made of pebbles set closely together. This could only have been done after the swampy ground had been drained, as Tarquin is supposed to have begun doing. Nor could a civic center have become important until after the ground had been paved.

Two years later Servius Tullius had to turn his attention away from the changes he was making in Rome, for unrest was again brewing in Veii, where Aulus Vibenna had gratefully dedicated his *bucchero* vase to Apollo. Since Vulci's revolt had not yet been quelled, it seemed a good time for Veii to press her claim to the saltworks at the mouth of the Tiber. And so, for the sixth time, Veii went to war against Rome. This time the war was to last twenty years.

During these years and indeed until the end of the sixth century, Etruria, with Rome playing an increasingly larger rôle, reached her widest expansion. She made great territorial gains, adding a large part of Campania, including Capua, and coming to blows from time to time with the Greek colonies in the south which were also expanding not only on the mainland but across the Tyrrhenian Sea to Corsica and Sardinia.

In 560 B.C. while the war with Veii was still in progress, with success veering from side to side (Livy and Dionysius of Halicarnassus assert that Rome won all the battles) Greek emigrants from Phocis near Smyrna came with their wives and children on their fifty-oared ships to Corsica and founded a city on the coast facing Italy, which they called Alalia. Here they built houses and temples and lived by raiding their neighbors.

In 540 B.C. these acts of piracy became unbearable, and the Etruscans joined with the Carthaginians to drive out the intruders. Each contributed sixty ships. The Phocaeans with twice as many ships, though they won the battle, lost fully two-thirds of their sea power and had to abandon Alalia. The crews of the broken Phocaean ships were captured, taken ashore near Cerveteri, and stoned to death. What part, if any, Servius Tullius and Rome had in the sea fight with the Phocaeans is not known. The twenty-year war with Veii had ended seven years after Alalia was founded, and Servius Tullius would have been free to share in the sea fight.

Just when Servius Tullius enlarged Rome by adding three more hills, the Esquiline, the Quirinal, and the Viminal is also unknown. Neither do we know when he transferred his palace to the Esquiline, nor when, according to some authorities, he built a circuit wall around the entire city. Careful examination, begun in 1932, of the building materials of the so-called Servian Wall, has removed all possibility that Servius can claim the whole of this important landmark in Rome's history. He can only be credited with having filled in the weak places in the city's natural defenses. Today, one such portion, patched and reinforced, stands near the handsome new railroad station in Rome.

A tradition, preserved by Livy, states that King Servius built on the Aventine Hill a temple to Diana, a goddess, like the Greek Artemis, of fertility and of childbirth. The previous headquarters of Diana's cult had been Aricia, near Lake Nemi, from which, in 1832, the Emperor Caligula's extravagant pleasure boats were raised. The tradition of a temple on the Aventine may have been an attempt, after the Latins had been conquered and amalgamated into Etruscan Rome, to remove the cult of Diana from Aricia, that the Latins might have a temple of their own. King Servius also had altars built for them in every quarter of the city.

The royal family in the palace on the Esquiline had for some years consisted of the widowed Tanaquil, Servius Tullius, his Queen, who was Tanaquil's daughter, and their two surviving daughters. The eldest girl, according to tradition, died in infancy. Tarquin and Tanaquil had had a son, but he had been killed in battle. He had left three orphaned children, a girl whose name seems to have been Tarquinia, and two boys, Lucius and Aruns.

These three children seem to have spent their early years with their grandmother in the palace on the Esquiline, but were later sent back to Tarquinia. The only children who remained in the palace were the small princesses, each named Tullia. Servius Tullius had followed Roman custom and given his daughters his own name. Since Livy calls one Tullia 'fiery,' perhaps the other sister had opposite characteristics. To distinguish between them, their parents may have followed the Roman custom, calling one Prima and the other Secunda.

At a critical moment in the reign of Servius Tullius history repeated itself; Tarquin's two grandsons, grown to young manhood, appeared in Rome. The education in Tarquinia of these two young princes, Lucius and Aruns, seems to have been mainly the usual study of the arts of divination from observation of the color and shape of a sheep's liver and from the flights of birds, as prescribed in the Tagetic Doctrine. Since the younger prince, Aruns, had shown greater aptitude for study, instruction in the art of government was added.

When Lucius and Aruns presented themselves at the palace on the Esquiline Hill, Servius Tullius, their uncle by marriage, invited them to live with his family, possibly because he felt secure enough to overlook the risk he might run from young ambitious noblemen. Or perhaps he was fully aware of the risk, and intended to counteract it in his own way. Whatever the reason, soon a double marriage occurred in the palace; Tullia Prima was given to Lucius, and Tullia Secunda to Aruns, an unfortunate arrangement, as Livy observes; for the 'fiery' princess was married to the elder but less ambitious of the two princes, and this situation carried within itself the seeds of an explosion.

Yet for a time, all seems to have gone well on the Esquiline Hill, where the two young couples lived with their aunt and uncle. Neither relative appears to have noticed that Tullia Prima had fixed envious eyes on her sister's husband. Livy records an imaginary conversation between Tullia Prima and Aruns in which

Prima upbraids her brother-in-law, taunting him with cowardice in not taking her away from her spineless husband.

Servius Tullius, like his predecessor, had no heir, and he must have longed for one. When his Queen passed beyond child-bearing age, he had only his two married daughters to pin his hopes upon. But time passed, and no offspring arrived to gladden his heart. One day—the date is unknown—Lucius, Prima's husband, died under mysterious circumstances. Not long afterward Tullia Secunda died an equally mysterious death. Shortly afterward, the surviving mates married.

The gods must have looked askance upon this hastily contrived marriage, for the girl who was born to the new couple did not long survive, and for some time no other child appeared. Finally the gods relented; a son was born to Aruns and Tullia. He was named Titus. Two more sons were born. One was named Aruns, the other Sextus. Later, a second daughter was born.

At about this time, or perhaps a little earlier, a Roman of noble family, whose name was Lucretius, had a daughter born to him. As Servius Tullius had done, Lucretius named his daughter after himself. Lucretia grew into a beautiful girl. When she came to marriageable age, perhaps fourteen, her family gave her to Lucius Tarquinius Collatinus, the son of Tarquin's nephew, Egerius, who had been appointed garrison commander of Collatia. By marriage, then, Lucretia became a member of the junior branch of the Tarquin family.

The public life of Servius Tullius seems to have been progressing smoothly enough, but in the palace on the Esquiline domestic matters were far from smooth. For, in spite of having obtained the man she wanted, and of having produced after that first disappointing daughter three sons, alive and sturdy, Tullia had not obtained her chief desire in life. She was not a queen. The thought of her grandmother's ability and clever political skill ate like a canker in her own ambitious spirit. Tanaquil had put two men on thrones: her husband, though he was the son of a foreigner, and her son-in-law, Tullia's own father.

Unable to endure any longer the indignity she felt so keenly, Tullia began to upbraid her husband, as she had done when he was her brother-in-law. She twitted him with his Greek blood, saying he was not worthy even of that. Day after day the bitter quarreling went on. Evil calls to evil, Livy writes. Certainly it seems that the evil in Tullia's heart must have roused the evil lying dormant in the heart of Aruns. He finally succumbed to his strong-minded wife and began to make his plans.

His grandfather had raised the number of the Senators to three hundred; in return they had given him their support. Now the patricians were discontented because Servius Tullius had favored the plebeians at their expense, and they resented deeply the loss of their privileges. To fan into flame the embers smoldering in the patrician hearts was a simple task for an ambitious young Etruscan noble and his wife.

When sure of patrician support, Aruns gathered together a band of hot-headed young followers, and with them at his back appeared in the Forum and boldly entered the Senate House. Standing before the unoccupied throne, Aruns charged the Senators with cowardice in suffering abuses at the hands of a monarch who did not even know his own parentage. He reminded them that Servius Tullius had never consulted the will of the people. Was Servius Tullius, he asked, a fit person to exact obedience from the patricians of Rome? Without waiting for an answer, Aruns seated himself upon the vacant throne.

The sound of a scuffle at the door drew all eyes. The King stood on the threshold. Aruns leaped up, strode down the aisle, seized the angry King, and threw him down the high steps. Half fainting, Servius got to his feet and staggered off alone. Aruns's young patricians followed him, killed him, and left his body lying on the ground.

Tullia, who seems to have known what Aruns meant to do, had driven to the Senate to be the first to pay her respects to the new ruler. Aruns saw her enter, and peremptorily ordered her home. When Tullia came to the place where her father's body lay, her slave driver pulled up his horses. With ashen face he turned to his mistress. She ordered him to drive over the body.

Aruns Tarquinius refused to allow the people to honor their dead king with a funeral that befitted his rank. He reminded them that their Romulus had had no funeral; he spoke with such vehemence that some one muttered *superbus*. The epithet fitted him and he became known as Tarquin the Proud.

The people disobeyed their new king. They erected in the Forum a wooden image with gilded face and painted eyes, and within sight of the image they placed the body of their beloved King Servius on its funeral pyre and applied the torch.

The middle of the sixth century B.C. had not yet arrived, yet already two Etruscan kings had suffered violent deaths in the City of the She-Wolf. Now a third had walked the bloody trail to the throne.

XV

Tarquin the Proud

(534 B.C. — 510 B.C.)

Two hundred and nineteen years after the founding of Rome, Tarquin the Proud became her third Etruscan king. The path to his grandfather's throne had been a trail of blood. His father had been killed in battle; his brother had died a mysterious death; his two predecessors had been murdered; and Tullia, his wife, the new Queen of Rome, not content with her father's death, had driven her chariot over his body.

But Tarquin's own crime had been worse; he had refused to allow Servius Tullius to be buried. This was an offense against the gods and the common people rebelled. To punish them for defying him, Tarquin immediately ordered all plebeian festivals to be discontinued, all Senators who had supported the late king put to death, and their property confiscated. History does not confirm the tradition that to make his own will supreme, Tarquin destroyed the fifty bronze placques on which Servius had had his new laws engraved. These laws, formulated and engraved after Tarquin's death, were probably destroyed much later, when toward the end of the fourth century B.C. the Gauls sacked Rome.

Had the placques existed in his day, Tarquin might well have destroyed them, since his subsequent acts showed that he had little respect for any rules except his own. Just as the entire reign of the first Tarquin had been a constant struggle against the liberal and democratic influence of his predecessor, Ancus Marcius, so now the second Tarquin tried to eradicate all traces of his own predecessor's democratic influence and re-establish the autocracy of his grandfather.

That Tarquin was really guilty of all the crimes he has been accused of is vouched for only by Roman writers, and they may not have been altogether impartial judges. They tell us that Tarquin made treaties with neighboring peoples and broke them at will, that he became a virtual dictator, and that no one dared withstand him. If all this is true, and if it is also true that he had been trained in Etruria, where political freedom was unknown, where power was in the hands of the nobles and the common people had no voice in government, to Tarquin such a system would be the only right and proper way to govern a people.

Prominent among the plebeians in Rome was a wealthy and reputable man, Marcus Junius, whose wife was a daughter of the first Tarquin. This Marcus Junius, his uncle by marriage, Tarquin is reputed to have put to death, either because he feared his opposition or because he needed his wealth to carry out the projects he had in mind. The death order included his uncle's two sons; one escaped, and eventually became the founder of republican Rome.

Perhaps the blood that ran in the streets of Rome during these early days of Tarquin's reign caused Tullia some remorse, for Livy reports that she went to the Temple of Fortuna, the Etruscan goddess whose cult her father had introduced into Rome, and that when she entered the temple and saw the gilded face of her father's statue, she turned aside and wept.

With the Etruscans and at first with the Latins Tarquin kept on good terms. He renewed the treaty with Veii—in the past it had been twice broken—that gave Rome control of the salt-works, and called to Rome skilled Etruscan artisans and painters to teach their arts to his Roman workmen. Soothsayers he also called in, and kept them near him, for this Tarquin, unlike his grandfather, was a credulous man. The Latins his predecessors had had such trouble with, he favored greatly, thinking, as Livy reports, that his strength abroad would contribute to his security at home. In pursuance of this policy, he gave his second daughter in marriage to a certain Mamilius Octavius, who was at that time the despotic ruler of the Latin town of Tusculum. Later on, when Tarquin was in need of friends, the relationship proved advantageous.

Because of this marriage and because of favors bestowed upon the Latins, Tarquin became so powerful that he could summon their leaders to an assembly whenever he wished. Livy has left an account of a meeting of the Latin League that was held at a place some call Feretina, others Feronia. Tarquin had ordered the League to meet there at dawn. The various heads of the Latin states arrived promptly, but Tarquin did not. After waiting for some time, a certain Turnus of Aricia, apparently the head of the League, rose and began to abuse Tarquin, in his absence, for having summoned them as if they were his vassals; he proposed that they should no longer wait. Toward sundown Tarquin appeared as Turnus was speaking. Turnus ceased abruptly, and the whole assembly fell silent. Tarquin explained his tardiness by saying he had had to arbitrate a quarrel between a father and his son. Turnus would not accept the explanation, railed at the Roman king more violently than before, and left the council.

That evening Tarquin set a trap for the rebellious chief from Aricia. He bribed one of Turnus's slaves to allow men to enter his master's tent during the night and hide a number of swords and other weapons. Assured that his orders had been carried out, Tarquin summoned another dawn meeting of all the leaders, except Turnus. Then he accused the absent chief of plotting not only against himself, but also against the other Latin heads of state, adding that he now understood why Turnus had been so vehement the day before.

"You will find in his tent full proof of what I am telling you," Tarquin told the astounded chiefs. "Follow me."

Unwillingly the chiefs followed Tarquin. They reached the tent while Turnus was still asleep. The slave who had been bribed led them to the place where the weapons were concealed. Outraged, the chiefs dragged Turnus from his bed, and giving him no time to explain or to defend himself, packed him in a wicker crate, weighted it with stones, and drowned him in the spring they had been in the habit of dipping their water from.

This was a new kind of death, Livy says.

Tarquin took advantage of the situation he had created to induce the Latin leaders to renew an old treaty that had fallen into abeyance. The treaty secured, Tarquin ignored the older men and summoned to a meeting all the young men of military age. So persuasively did he talk to them of the new alliance their elders had made with him that when he explained the advantages of fighting under his leadership, no one offered any objection. Tarquin then broke up their military formations and mingled the young Latins with his own legions.

With his reinforced army, Tarquin moved against Vulci, the city that had rebelled against his grandfather. Nothing is known of the attack except that the city seems to have succumbed easily, perhaps because Tarquin had overcome Vulci's traditional enemies, the Latins. The booty Tarquin acquired from Vulci, he sold for an enormous sum—Livy does not say who bought it—and set aside the money to complete the temple his grandfather had vowed to build on the Capitoline Hill in Rome.

To make room for his temple, Tarquin ordered several small shrines destroyed. The work proceeded according to plan, since the birds, whose will had been consulted, apparently did not object to the desecration. But when the workmen began to remove a shrine consecrated to the god Terminus, the birds refused their consent. Just how the birds manifested their displeasure is unknown. Probably the soothsayers reported that they had seen the birds fly to the inauspicious left, and explained to King Tarquin that the refusal to allow him to remove so ancient a shrine as that of the god Terminus meant that Rome would always remain strong and steadfast.

Leaving the shrine of Terminus untouched, Tarquin set out to attack Gabii, a Latin town some sixteen miles east of Rome, the present Castiglione. But Gabii was well-fortified and had no intention of submitting to an Etruscan king. Unable to take the town by assault and disturbed by losing so many of his men, Tarquin resorted to trickery. He pretended to abandon the siege, said that he must oversee the men who were digging on the site of his new temple, and with part of his army marched back to Rome, leaving encamped near the stubborn town his youngest son, Sextus, to carry out the trick he had planned.

In Rome a shock awaited him. His workmen, though plebeians, were Roman citizens and they were being forced to do manual labor that belonged properly to slaves. When the King appeared, they showed him a human head, intact, which they had dug up on the site he planned for his temple. Completely unnerved by the prodigy, Tarquin asked advice of the Etruscan soothsayers he always kept near him. When they explained that the omen meant "here would be the head of the world," he dismissed his fears and decided to use the state funds in order to build a more magnificent temple than he had originally planned.

Apparently Rome could not supply Tarquin with the labor he now needed, for he had men brought in from all Etruria. He also ordered made in Veii a terra-cotta *quadriga* (four-horse chariot) to decorate in Etruscan fashion the temple pediment. But in the furnace the clay swelled and broke the mold, and the sculptors could not get the chariot out. This was interpreted as "increase of dominion to the possessor," and so the chariot remained in Veii. Shortly afterward, in Veii a victor in a chariot race was leaving the arena when his horses took fright and dashed off toward

Rome. At the foot of the Capitol, the horses stampeded, threw out their driver, and killed him. Frightened by the portent, the Veientes quickly made another chariot, and presented it to Tarquin.

Dennis reminds his readers that the *quadriga* was among the "seven sacred things, on the preservation of which the power and safety of Rome were believed to depend." He lists the other six: the Palladium (brought by Aeneas from Troy), Cybele's needle, the ashes of Orestes, Priam's scepter, Ilione's veil, and the Salian shields.

While Tarquin was preparing to decorate his temple with the newly-arrived *quadriga*, Sextus, who had been left behind to trick the stubborn town of Gabii into submission, was telling the people a pitiful story, that he had fled to them to escape from his cruel father, who was plotting to kill all three of his sons. If the people of Gabii would grant him asylum, Sextus told them, he would divulge to them his father's entire plan. At first the leaders of the people did not believe him, but Sextus was so plausible that they were finally convinced. They assured Sextus that his skill in warfare could be useful to them; with his help they might even lay siege to Rome. Sextus played his cards well; when he was made a member of their council he deferred modestly to the advice of his elders, adamant upon only one point, that war alone would save them, and that they must take the initiative while his father's mind was upon the great temple he was building. Soon Sextus prevailed upon the leaders of Gabii to give him a command of young men, eager to prove themselves in warfare. With their support, he then carried out a few skirmishes with the besiegers to display his skill in routing an enemy. Enthusiasm for their new commander rose when other skirmishes with the Romans invariably turned out to be successes for Gabii. Soon, upon the insistence of the army, Sextus became their commander-in-chief.

When Sextus decided that his position and his military strength warranted the next move, he sent a messenger to his father in Rome. Tarquin received the messenger in his garden. As if unable to give an answer, the King walked up and down in silence, the messenger following, while Tarquin, as though absent-minded, kept striking off the heads of the tallest poppies near him. Perplexed and angered, the messenger returned to Sextus and told what he had seen. Sextus understood. At once he set to work to get rid of the leaders of Gabii. Some he accused to the people, who ordered them executed and their property confiscated; some he himself put to death secretly; others he allowed to go into exile. Since all confiscated property, including often the newly-made widows and their marriageable daughters, was turned over to the people, all sense of decency was quickly lost in the general corruption. The result of this maneuvering was that when Tarquin himself appeared to lay siege again to the town, no one resisted him. And so after seven years, another Latin town passed into Tarquin's hands.

While the great temple on the Capitoline Hill was still under construction, Tarquin set the plebeians to even more laborious tasks. The Circus his predecessor had built to entertain the populace with games still had no seats. Spectators had to bring their own. A painting from the Tomb of the Augurs in Tarquinia, dated about 530 B.C., shows a stalwart man, dressed in the usual high-backed boots and draped mantle, beckoning to his slave to hurry along with the stool he carries on his shoulder. Obviously no common man, as his mantle and boots (as sharply pointed as his beard) indicate, he may be, as some scholars think, an umpire hastening to the games.

The seats the new Circus needed, Tarquin now set a force of unwilling plebeians to build. Other plebeians he set to work upon an immense underground sewer that was to receive the drainage from the ditches Tarquin the Elder and Servius Tullius had had dug to carry off the swamp water. The grumbling of those who were assigned to dig the Great Sewer may have reached the royal ears. Whatever the cause, on the pretext that there was no longer enough work for all, the King dispatched the grumblers as colonists to Etruria's most remote frontiers.

In 524 B.C., because he still needed money to carry out his plans for Rome, Tarquin attacked the Greek city, Cumae, from which the old woman had come with the Sibylline books she sold to Tarquin the Elder. But Tarquin the Proud had not reckoned, in this tenth year of his reign, with a certain Aristodemus, an ambitious Greek in the city, who saw in the Etruscan siege an opportunity to better his own position among his fellows. We have no details of his battle against the attacking Etruscans, only that Tarquin and his well-trained army were repulsed. This was the first defeat of Tarquin the Proud.

It may have been about this time that Tarquin began to be troubled by ominous dreams: a pair of eagles had built a nest in a palm tree in his garden and had hatched two eaglets. One day when the parents returned with food for their young, they found the eaglets gone and a pair of vultures in possession. Tarquin dreamed again: two rams, from the same father's seed, were brought to him for sacrifice. When he selected one, the other ram butted the chosen one away from the altar. Then a report came that the sun had changed its course.

Shortly afterward a terrible portent appeared to Tarquin himself. The pillars of his palace on the Esquiline Hill were made of wood. Out of one of these pillars a serpent glided, paused with head erect, then slipped away through the palace. No one dared pursue the serpent, for fear that under this guise the old king might have returned to avenge his death, or that he had sent it to warn the royal house of coming evil.

Unable to learn from his Etruscan soothsayers what these dreams and portents meant—the soothsayers merely warned the King to beware of a man "of his own blood and as stupid as a sheep"—Tarquin sent a mission to Delphi in Greece. The mission consisted of his two eldest sons, Titus and Aruns, and with them his sister's son, Marcus Lucius Junius, whom he had taken into his own family and had nicknamed Brutus, thinking him a stupid oaf.

Arrived in Delphi, the royal messengers performed the required sacrifices, asked the questions Tarquin had bidden them put to the oracle, and then put one of their own:

"Which of us shall be king in Rome?"

"He who shall be the first to kiss his mother," came the answer.

Tradition adds that the two young princes drew lots to decide which should be the first to kiss the Queen, their mother. Tradition also adds that Brutus, the supposed dullard, had brought along with him as his offering to the oracle his own official staff—Brutus was a Tribune of the Plebs—its hollow interior filled with gold.

As the three young men were leaving the sanctuary, Brutus pretended to stumble. He landed on the ground on all fours—and pressed his lips to the earth.

"The Earth is our mother," he told his companions. One wonders if Brutus had used the gold in his staff to obtain more instruction from the oracle than his kinsmen had—for the young men had entered singly into the shrine. If he had, his conduct hardly corresponds to his later stern integrity.

In 513 B.C. when Tarquin had been on the throne twenty-one years, the Etruscans crossed the Apennines and descended into the Po valley. Here they founded Felsina (Bologna), and reaching the Adriatic Sea, established trading-posts which later became flourishing Etruscan cities. Whether Tarquin himself took part in these ventures is not known; probably he was still occupied with the troublesome Latin cities near Rome.

Livy tells us that when Tarquin attacked another Latin stronghold, Ardea, an important port city and no great distance from Rome, he put Sextus, the son who had captured Gabii for him, in charge of a division composed of Latins and Etruscans. Ardea held out against Tarquin longer than anyone had expected, and after a while Sextus and the other young officers became bored. Some one suggested a hunt in the nearby forest. The day went off well, for the young men hunted in the Etruscan fashion, using musical instruments to attract the animals within reach of their weapons. That evening the hunters feasted royally, meat and wine being plentiful.

Soon they began to cast about for other entertainment. The night was young, the air soft and pleasant, and the officers flushed with meat and the day's excitement. All except Sextus, who was a bachelor, fell to talking about their absent wives, wondering how they were amusing themselves in their lonely homes. The talk turned on chastity.

Among the officers with Sextus was his cousin, Lucius Tarquinius Collatinus, whose wife was the beautiful Lucretia. When each man began to extol the chastity of his own wife, the loudest voice among them was that of Collatinus. Finally some one propo·ed that they should all ride to Rome and surprise their wives. The proposal was greeted with enthusiasm, and the officers set out for Rome. There they went directly to the palace on the Esquiline Hill, where they found Queen Tullia and her ladies at a banquet. Seated on high couches around the banquet table, they were watching the acrobats, clowns, and dancers Tullia had summoned to entertain her guests. No men were present.

From the innocent palace revels the officers accompanied Collatinus to his home in nearby Collatia. They arrived at night and found Lucretia spinning wool with her slave women. Lucretia received her unexpected visitors graciously and seconded her husband's invitation to them to remain and enjoy an evening meal. During the meal the sight of the young matron of whose chastity her husband had boasted roused in Sextus the desire to possess her for himself. A few days later, accompanied by a slave attendant, Sextus returned to Collatia. Upon what pretext he was admitted to the house, Livy, who tells the story, does not say. But Sextus was Tarquin's son, and a kinsman, and Lucretia could have suspected no harm. After the evening meal he was shown to a guest chamber. When the house had settled to its sleep, Sextus rose and, sword in hand, made his way through the dark to Lucretia's room. Shakespeare, who has immortalized the story in *The Rape of Lucrece,* pictures the frightened girl looking with horrified eyes at the intruder.

With his left hand Sextus pushed her down on her bed; with his right he held his sword at her throat and began to plead his love. Lucretia refused. He threatened her with death. Still she refused. He threatened to dishonor her, kill his slave, and place him naked beside her dead body; her husband would believe her caught in adultery with a slave.

Lucretia yielded.

The next morning Lucretia dispatched two messengers: one to her father Lucretius, who was in Rome, the other to her husband at Ardea. To each she sent the same message: to choose a trusted friend and come at once to Collatia. Lucretius brought his friend Valerius with him. Collatinus, who was on his way to Rome when his wife's messenger reached him, selected Marcus Junius, called Brutus, who had stumbled at Delphi and kissed the earth. The four men found Lucretia sitting alone in her chamber. Calmly she told them what had happened and exacted a pledge from each man to avenge her. Then she revealed the name of her violator. Astounded and horrified, her listeners tried to comfort her, pointing out that she had been under duress and that she had committed no wrong.

"I can no longer live," Lucretia replied, and before anyone could stop her, she plunged her dagger into her heart.

Brutus drew out the dagger, and swore upon it never to rest until he had driven the accursed Tarquins out of Rome. Then each man placed his hand upon the sword and, one by one, swore the oath. They carried Lucretia's body to the marketplace and left it there with her grief-stricken father on guard. Brutus and Collatinus, at the head of a rapidly increasing force of armed and angry men, set off for Rome. No one else was allowed to leave Collatia, lest the news of armed men marching on Rome reach the ears of Tarquin and his sons. But the story ran ahead, and when Brutus arrived, he found the Forum packed.

Brutus did not mince his words. He reminded his listeners of all the wrongs they had suffered at the hands of Tarquin the Proud: the shameful murder of Servius Tullius, the outrageous behavior of Tullia, and now the violation of Lucretia, who had chosen death rather than live in dishonor. Fully roused, the people shouted for an end to the monarchy; Tarquin and all his family must be driven from Rome. Young men gathered around Brutus, volunteering to serve under him if he would lead them against Tarquin at Ardea. During the general confusion, Tullia managed to escape from the city. Where she found refuge Livy does not say. She probably went to Cerveteri, since that was the city where Tarquin and two of his sons finally arrived.

Before Brutus and his men reached Ardea, Tarquin had learned of his son's action. Cicero reports that Tarquin merely blamed his son for his poor judgment in selecting a member of one of the most powerful families in Rome, when he could have satisfied his lust upon a common woman. Finally convinced that the situation was serious, Tarquin and his two eldest sons took the Etruscan soldiers —the Romans and the Latins had defected at once—and started off to quell the revolt in Rome. A surprise awaited them. The gates of Rome were closed and guarded. A representative of the people stood on the walls and read aloud the sentence of banishment.

Tarquin marched his men to Cerveteri. There he heard that Sextus had gone to Gabii, and that the citizens he had betrayed had put him to death. These events occurred in 510 B.C., two years before the great temple on the Capitoline Hill was dedicated, not to the Etruscan Tinia as planned, but to the Roman Jupiter. Tarquin the Proud, the third Etruscan king of Rome, was in exile, plotting his return.

Some scholars dismiss the story of Lucretia's violation and suicide as an outgrowth of popular poetry. Alain Hus suggests that Roman tradition disguised the expulsion of the Tarquins as an affair of honor, but that the real cause was a "national uprising against foreign occupation." This agrees with the view of de Coulanges, who considers the story as part of the struggle between dictatorial power and patrician control, comparable to what was happening at this period elsewhere in the Mediterranean world, where social revolutions had begun to brew.

Etruscan society, built upon the authority of the *lucumo*, who was both king and priest, had reached the point where the kingly function overshadowed that of the priest. At Rome before the first Tarquin came, the patrician Senate had always chosen the king from their own ranks, but on all important matters, both political and religious, the king was expected to consult his peers.

The first Tarquin flouted the patrician Senate and gained the throne by the help of the plebeians. The authority of the ancient families meant no more to him than did their religion. He changed what he did not like. He was murdered.

Tarquin's successor, Servius Tullius, mounted the throne at Tanaquil's behest. The Senate never recognized him. He took property away from the patricians and gave it to the plebeians, conferred political rights upon them, and made them members of the armed forces. From this time on the struggle was between the king and the people on the one side and the patricians, who stood for the old order, on the other side. This meant that the patricians were caught in a squeeze between King Servius in front of them and the lower classes, whom they despised, rising up behind them. Servius Tullius was murdered.

The second Tarquin argued his rights so strongly before the Senate that they elected him; he was a nobleman and therefore one of their own kind. He disappointed them; he lopped off heads with equanimity; he consulted no one but himself; he became a dictator.

The patricians waited their chance; it came, tailored to their choice. Tarquin was absent on his wars; the city was in the hands of its prefect, Lucretius, the patrician. The commander of the cavalry was Marcus Junius, who was also, according to Dionysius, a patrician. These two men, as de Coulanges puts together the scattered pieces of the story, formed a conspiracy. With two trusted associates, Valerius and Lucius Tarquinius Collatinus, they went to the little town of Collatia, where they exhibited the body of a woman who, they said, had committed suicide because she had been violated by a king's son.

The conspirators then moved on to Rome and repeated the same scene and the same story. The Senate issued a decree of banishment against Tarquin and his sons. An assembly of the people was quickly convened, the matter laid before them, and the names of the two men proposed who were to act as consuls of the new Republic of Rome.

Whichever interpretation of the story is true, the expulsion of the Tarquins and the consequent loss of Rome to Etruria contributed its share to her eventual disappearance as an ethnic entity. Whether this was even hinted at in the Tagetic Doctrine no one except the great god Tinia, or perchance Voltumna, the god of the sacred Grove, could have known.

XVI

The God of the Sacred Grove

On a hill top in the territory of Volsinia a little distant from the modern town of Orvieto, renowned for its wine, a pine grove stands in dark, brooding silence. Monte Falcone, the peasants now call the hill, but what its name was in Etruscan days no one knows. Perhaps it had no name. It was the Grove, the sacred Grove where a god dwelt in lonely majesty.

At the foot of the hill a lake shimmers, celestial blue when the weather is fine, as it nearly always is in this region of Etruria. The pines on the hill top are very old, possibly old enough to recall that once the Grove was sacred to a god Voltumna, to whom men told a mysterious and at that time an easily credible tale, that the god of the sacred Grove possessed a dual nature. "Dress me in Coan silk," the Latin poet Propertius imagines Voltumna saying, "and I shall be a tender maiden. If I wear a toga, who shall deny that I am a man?"

Dennis thinks Voltumna was a goddess and the wife of the god Vertumnus, the Etruscan Bacchus, with whose help the volcanic soil of the region produced the vine. Von Vacano does not mention Propertius, but he interprets the tradition the poet refers to as indicating that Voltumna was a bi-sexual god and that the cult in the Grove must have been "a very ancient one."

Whoever or whatever the deity, no one doubts that the Grove was the most important religious shrine of Etruria. Once a year, many people, coming from all the Etruscan cities round about, brought gifts, and afterward remained to talk over with one another affairs common to them all.

The centuries passed. The eighth gave way to the seventh; the seventh to the sixth, and the sixth brought the loss of Rome to Etruria's men of bronze, who found it hard to believe they had lost their foothold across the Tiber. Harder yet was it to believe that Tarquin the Proud was nursing his wounded pride in Cerveteri. As for Tullia, his wicked Queen, the less said about her the better. So men talked, gathered again at year's end in the Grove on the hill top to watch the sacred ceremony, the great wooden year-nail being driven slowly home.

As usual, the twelve member cities had sent their leaders, a patrician *lucumo* from each city, and, as usual, the twelve had chosen one of their number to act as Head and drive the year-nail into the temple wall, but this time men sensed an uneasiness in the air and strove to learn from the soothsayers what fresh evil the god had in store for the Union of the Rasenna, as those who assembled in the Grove liked to call themselves.

The Union of the Rasenna, as all Etruria knew, was an organization for religious purposes only; it was not intended to be a military alliance of the cities, each pledged to go to another's defense; and it meant to keep its old character, no matter how often Tarquin and his sons there in Cerveteri urged the cities to go to war against the new Roman Republic—a political entity that no one understood, and that they feared as something unknown. So the talk ran that year in the Grove when melancholy was settling down over Etruria because Tarquin the Proud had been read out of Rome.

When the Union, or confederation, of the Rasenna, was formed in Central Etruria is not known, since archaeology has not yet been able to determine the age of the shrine, nor whether the god Voltumna had always been worshiped in the same place. But with this problem the Union was not concerned.

163

Some scholars feel that the Etruscan cities of Campania in southern Italy were the first to form a federation with Capua as its center. If the late Roman historian Velleius Paterculus, who was of Campanian descent, may be relied upon, the Etruscans founded Capua forty-seven years before Rome's traditional date of 753 B.C.

The original inhabitants of Campania had been the Oscans, but Greek colonies from overseas had driven them out and had settled Cumae. Then along came Etruscans who founded Capua as a foil to the Greek Cumae, whose reputation as the home of the oracular Sibyl had greatly enhanced its reputation throughout Campania.

The discovery at Capua of the terra-cotta tile with Etruscan writing on it has now been generally accepted as evidence that the city was Etruscan, or rather, an assemblage of people who became united because they spoke the same language and worshiped the same gods.

Rome, at any rate, could not at that time have been a barrier to Etruscan expansion in Campania, but the Oscans were, for they went inland and founded Pompeii at the mouth of the river Liris. The Oscans were not left in peace long; the men in bronze could not be withstood, and Pompeii soon became Etruscan, to remain so until Rome, also expanding southward, drove them out and following her usual custom sent in colonies, this time made up of retired legionaries.

No agreement has yet been reached about the identity of the twelve Etruscan cities that composed the Union of the Rasenna nor why the name Rasenna was applied to the confederation in Central Etruria and not to that in Campania, nor to the confederation that was formed, later on, when the Etruscans moved northward, to center around Mantua. Some scholars have solved the puzzle by denying the existence of any federation except that in central Etruria. They may be right.

Though scholars disagree as to which twelve cities composed the Union of the Rasenna, no one any longer asserts that Rome was ever a member. The suggestion has been made that she may have once been an "associate member," doubtless because tradition connects the name of one of the Tarquins with the organization of the Union, but not with its establishment. Toward the end of Etruria's independence the twelve cities were Arrezzo, Cerveteri, Chiusi, Cortona, Perugia, Populonia, Rosellae, Tarquinia, Vetulonia, Volsinia, Volterra, and Vulci. The membership may, of course, have been changed from time to time. This would account for the striking omission of Veii, the city that fought so long and courageously against Roman domination.

Though Tarquinia may have been the capital of the Union of Rasenna, its annual meetings were held in the Grove near ancient Volsinia, whose precise location was in doubt until 1946 when Raymond Bloch was authorized to examine Monte Falcone. His discovery of part of a long wall, a burial-ground, a rock temple, and a fortified section, proved that a city had once stood there. Whether Monte Falcone was actually the site of the Grove where a bi-sexual god held sway does not matter so much as the character of the annual meetings and their importance for Etruria.

The chief duty of the head *lucumo* was the ceremonial driving of the year-nail into the wall of the inner sanctuary of the temple of Nortia, the goddess of destiny, who is generally equated with the Greek Atropos (she from whom there is no turning). But driving a nail into a wall "symbolized," von Vacano writes, "the acceptance of the inevitability of divine fate," which was believed to govern all events, or perhaps, as Mayani thinks, to "nail down" misfortune. Von Vacano adds that Horace "makes Necessitas, companion of the Etruscan *Fortuna* of Praeneste (Palestrina), carry wood-nails and bronze axe-heads in her hands." For religion, everywhere, is conservative, and so wood and bronze were sacred because they belonged to the old religion. Iron was forbidden: it was new and therefore evil.

At the Grove, after the sacred ceremony of the year-nail had been witnessed, the gathering took on the air of a festival, easily imagined by any one who has watched a country fair. It was even pleasanter in old Mediterranean days, when people had no newspapers and few other means of communication. For the latest news, gossip, or scandal people at the Grove knew they would have to rely upon the itinerant traders, who were, no doubt, a constant feature at the meetings. Pleasantest of all were the acrobatic stunts, the wrestling-matches, and the prize-fights, cheering on the champion from one's own city and celebrating his victory with a beaker of wine.

Now that the Tiber had again become the barrier to Etruscan expansion in southern Italy either by land or by sea, since Rome held the land routes and Cumae, by defeating Tarquin's forces, held the ports, Etruria turned her face toward the northern valleys of the Apennines. From there word drifted back to the Grove of new conquests, new settlements, new openings for commercial development; and men's spirits revived. But the revolution of the common people at Rome that had driven out the Tarquins was beginning to have its repercussions in Etruria, and men whispered, too low for the patrician *lucumones* to hear, that perhaps, just perhaps, King Porsenna of Chiusi might assist Tarquin to regain his throne. Then Rome would again become an Etruscan stronghold.

It was a dream, and men knew it; but they also knew that sometimes dreams come true. They knew, too, that even if Rome had declared herself forever free of the Etruscan yoke she had borne since the days of the first Tarquin, all was not well in the City of the She-Wolf. The new republican government was headed by two men, each to be a check upon the other. They were known as consuls and they were to hold office for one year only, an unheard of arrangement in those days of kings and soothsayers. The first consul elected was Brutus, who had sworn vengeance upon the Tarquins; the second was Collatinus, whose wife Lucretia had been violated by Sextus and had chosen death rather than dishonor. The consuls would be preceded by lictors, bearing aloft the Etruscan insignia of royal power, the rods and the axes, the *fasces*. It would not be easy to overthrow men who had once tasted such power.

Soon the Grove heard that Brutus had brought the number of the Senators back up to three hundred, appointed a priest to take charge of the public sacrifices—this duty had belonged to the kings—and obliged the people to swear a solemn oath never again to permit any man to be king. Brutus had then gone so far as to point out that Collatinus, his fellow-consul, belonged to the junior branch of the Tarquin family and that he might be receptive if his exiled kinsman should make overtures to him. One by one, all avenues of approach to the restoration of the monarchy were being closed, and hope waned again.

For some *lucumones* who came to the annual meetings at the Grove, the separation from southern Italy, particularly from Crotona, where the Greek Pythagoras had founded his religious brotherhood, was a spiritual hardship. Many of them, believing that Pythagoras was a brother of Tyrrhenus, had ordered their private lives according to the rules and the secret signs observed by members of the brotherhood. Their belief that the soul was divine and lived in the body as in a prison from which it constantly sought to escape attracted other *lucumones;* but they found it difficult to reconcile such an idea with their own Tagetic Doctrine, that a man became, eventually, a god. The discrepancy between the two beliefs afforded material for endless enjoyable discussions.

Matters of everyday life intruded, for instance, the disquieting news from Rome that the consul Collatinus had finally succumbed to pressure from Brutus and had resigned his office, merely because he was related to the Tarquins. In his stead Publius Valerius had been elected, that same Valerius who had conspired with the patrician Lucretius to overthrow the Tarquins.

On the heels of that election came a report from Cerveteri that Tarquin had sent messengers to Rome to lay a request before the Senate. Taken at face value, the request appeared modest and reasonable, but to worried Etruscans, it seemed that Tarquin was relinquishing his claim to the throne and to everything the Tagetic Doctrine taught.

The Tarquins had asked that their personal possessions be restored. The issue threw the Senate into a turmoil. In spite of strong consular objection, those who favored granting the request persuaded the more recalcitrant members to vote in the affirmative. No one knew then that the messengers were playing a double game. They had brought letters to friends of the royal family urging that arrangements be made to bring the Tarquins at night and secretly into Rome.

The Senate, in granting the family request for the return of their personal possessions, had also granted the messengers' request for a suitable length of time in which to collect the necessary vehicles for the transportation to Cerveteri. During the time allowed, Tarquin sent letters to his patrician friends in the city to assure them they could trust his messengers.

Tarquin's friends held their final meeting at the house of one of their members. They discussed their plot at the dinner table, and decided that the vehicles they had now collected in a safe place could be used to bring the royal family secretly into the city. An attending slave overheard the table conversation and reported it to the consuls. The dreaded lictors arrived and seized the messengers with the incriminating letters.

With the letters in their possession, the consuls rounded up the conspirators and threw them into prison. Among them were relatives of Brutus himself, his nephews and his two sons. All were sentenced to death. Since the messengers were citizens of a foreign country, as Etruria was now regarded, and could not be punished, they were sent back to Cerveteri. The Senate hastily rescinded its promise to restore the personal possessions of the royal family. Instead of selling off what the palace contained and putting the money in the public treasury, as many Senators urged, the consuls announced that the people might plunder the palace.

The Tarquins owned a stretch of land between the city and the Tiber. This land was now seized and consecrated to the Roman war god Mars. A crop of wheat growing on the land was ready to be harvested, but since the wheat belonged to Mars, it could not be eaten. The entire crop was, accordingly, cut close to the ground, carried off in baskets, and given to the Tiber. The summer had been dry, and the Tiber low, and so the stalks of wheat floated sluggishly down stream and soon, where the currents met, formed an island.

On the day appointed for carrying out the death sentence upon the conspirators, they were taken from prison and brought before the assembled people in the Forum. Each man, including Brutus's sons, was tied to a stake. The twelve lictors appeared, each with his bundle of rods and axes. Brutus and his fellow-consul followed; they took their places on the high tribunal, facing the condemned youths. Brutus, his face twisted in anguish, gave the order.

The lictors unbound the prisoners, stripped them, and scourged them. Then they beheaded them.

Rome murmured. The sound swelled and reached the sacred Grove, where people talked loudly and boldly, feeling that the time had come to retake Rome and seat Tarquin the Proud again upon his throne.

Rome had murmured against the treatment Brutus had meted out to his own sons; but the murmuring in the Grove resounded throughout Etruria when men heard that the Etruscan temple on the Capitoline Hill was to be dedicated to the Roman Jupiter. Henceforth he, a Roman god, and not Etruscan Tinia, would dwell in the holy central shrine, flanked by Juno and Minerva, each in her shrine, instead of the Etruscan goddesses, Cupra and Menrva.

Against this desecration, all Etruria waited for a sign of Tinia's displeasure. None came.

PART FOUR
THE IRON AGE

"For now truly is a race of iron . . . and the gods shall lay sore trouble upon them . . ."

HESIOD, *Works and Days*

XVII

Tarquin's Last Effort Fails

The rumor that the great temple on the Capitoline Hill was soon to be dedicated, not to the mighty Tinia of the Etruscans, but to the false Jupiter of the Romans, undoubtedly increased Tarquin's angry resentment against Brutus and the Roman Senate for denying him his rightful property. Though well advanced in age—he had reigned twenty-four years—Tarquin decided to make a strong effort to regain his throne. He reminded his two surviving sons, Aruns and Titus, of the prophecy the Roman and Etruscan soothsayers had made, that where the "intact head" had been found would be the head of the world.

Livy writes that Tarquin the Proud, as a suppliant who had never before assumed such a rôle, went about among the Etruscan cities, persuading them to war. Two cities responded, Tarquinia and Veii, both eager to punish the ungrateful Romans whose city the Tarquins had raised from the waters of a swamp.

Jubilant over his success, and with the armed fighting-men of two cities under his command, Tarquin crossed the Tiber and invaded Roman territory. He ordered Aruns to lead with the horsemen. He himself would follow with the foot soldiers. Livy does not say what position Titus was to hold nor what part he took in the battle.

Aruns, riding at the head of his horsemen, saw in the distance a detachment of Roman cavalry galloping across the plain toward him. As they came nearer, he recognized the consular lictors with their rods and axes. Then he recognized Brutus. Shouting to his men to follow, Aruns spurred on his horse and dashed straight for Brutus, the man whom he held responsible for his family's wrongs. With a clash of metal, they came together. Each thrust his spear with such force that it went through his opponent's shield, and could not be pulled loose. Impaled upon each other's spears, Aruns the Etruscan, and Brutus his Roman kinsman, fell under the feet of their frantic horses.

Swords and battle-axes flashing in the sunshine, Etruscans and Romans charged each other. Arrows whizzed overhead, and found their mark; spears flew, and under the slash of battle-axes heads rolled upon the ground. Soon nothing could be heard except the clash of metal, the screams of wounded horses, and the cries of trampled men. The Etruscan right drove back the Roman left, but its own left had to give way, the men from Veii first. Tarquin held fast, and even forced the Romans to give ground. Though by the end of the day the battle was still not decided, panic drove the Etruscans and their allies to quit the field.

Livy reports a prodigy: Publius Valerius, who had led the Roman foot soldiers, remained on the field throughout the night. The next morning, since no enemy was to be seen, he gathered up the "spoils," obviously including his colleague's body, though Livy does not mention that detail, and returned to Rome to celebrate the funeral. After Valerius had gone and night was falling, some one reported hearing a voice from the forest near by: "The Etruscans have lost one more man than the Romans have, therefore the Romans have conquered."

At Rome the people mourned Brutus, the women for a full year, so great was their grief for the man who had avenged "female modesty." What happened in Cerveteri when Tarquin returned with the body of his dead son, Livy does not say.

For a time Valerius, the surviving consul, stood alone without a colleague, whether by necessity or by design, no one seems to have recorded. Soon the people began to suspect him of planning to restore the monarchy, not for Tarquin, but for himself. The only grounds for suspicion appear to have been that Valerius was building a house in a section of the Capitoline Hill called the Velia, a position of natural strength that could be turned into a fort.

To defend himself against growing suspicion, Valerius called a general assembly. Preceded by his lictors, who held their *fasces* inverted, Valerius mounted the podium and in a voice of passionate conviction reminded the people that he had always been a bitter opponent of monarchy, and that, since he had lost his reputation for so trivial a cause as building a house on the Velia, he would immediately give orders to have his house rebuilt on lower ground; he would even have it built "under a hill" rather than incur so baseless a suspicion.

This episode is worth remembering because Livy is at pains to call attention to the joy of the people when they saw the inverted *fasces,* and realized that at last their revolution had borne fruit. They were the masters of Rome. Valerius then had laws passed granting the right of appeal against the decision of a magistrate, and calling for a curse to be pronounced upon the life and property of any man who plotted to become king.

Finally the people elected a second consul to hold office jointly with Valerius, who by this time had moved his house down to the foot of the hill. The new consul's name was Horatius.

In 508 B.C. the great temple was ready to be dedicated. Horatius and Valerius drew lots for the honor and Horatius won. Unwilling to accept the decision, Valerius's friends tried everything they could think of to put off the dedication. Finally at the solemn moment when Horatius, his hand on the temple door, had begun his prayer, a messenger rushed up and told him that his son was dead, and with death in his house he could not dedicate a temple.

Horatius listened; keeping his hold on the door, he gave the order for his son to be buried, then completed his prayer, and dedicated the temple.

In Cerveteri, Tarquin brooded in silent rage. But he was not the man to remain long inactive. He took Titus with him, and went to Chiusi to consult King Porsenna. Now at this period in Etruscan history Chiusi was one of the most powerful, some say *the* most powerful, of the twelve cities in the Union of Rasenna. According to the Roman historian Polybius, the ancient city then called Clusium was three days' journey from Rome, or approximately one hundred miles.

Porsenna, a generous-hearted man, seems to have taken a fancy to young Titus. Whether this influenced him, or whether Tarquin's persuasive eloquence had its effect, the historians do not say. Among other arguments that Tarquin advanced and that Porsenna must have listened to was that the institution of monarchy was the noblest effort of man. The growing custom of expelling kings must be stopped, and the rabble in Rome forced to realize that men could not be expected to know how to govern themselves. Unless Porsenna upheld the god-given rights of a fellow-monarch, chaos would rule Etruria.

With an allied army at his back, for other cities listened to Tarquin, among them Tarquinia and Veii, Porsenna took the field, intending to starve Rome into submission. "Never before," Livy writes, "had such great terror struck the Senate."

Fearing that the Roman people, sick of war, would throw open the city gates to the Etruscans, the Senate bought up large supplies of grain and brought it secretly into the city. The salt-monopoly, long in private hands, was returned to the government. Prices fell to a satisfactory level. The Senate next freed the plebeians from all taxation; the poor paid enough to the state by raising children, the Senate announced when the outraged patricians objected to shouldering the extra taxes.

When the Etruscans appeared on their side of the Tiber, the Roman peasants left their fields and flocked into the city. But instead of trying to cross the wooden bridge Ancus Marcius had had built on piles in the river, Porsenna attacked the Janiculum Hill, no longer the unfortified place it had been when the lady Tanaquil interpreted the omen of the eagles to her Lucumo.

Frightened out of all sense, when they saw Porsenna's dreaded standard at their gates, Janiculum's defenders surrendered at once and fled down the hill, throwing away their arms as they ran, while the triumphant Etruscans raced at their heels.

At the entrance to the bridge stood a lone sentinel, Horatius Cocles. Toward him the fleeing Romans charged, one thought in every head, to cross the bridge into the safety of their own land. Horatius barred their flight. Somehow he made his panic-stricken countrymen understand what they had to do, cut or fire the bridge behind him; he would hold the enemy at bay until they had finished.

There at the head of the wooden bridge he stood, Horatius Cocles, armed with sword and shield, alone, facing the Etruscan spears, while the bridge wavered and crackled behind him.

Two shamed Romans turned back to join him. When scarcely anything was left of the bridge, Horatius ordered his companions to save themselves. Again he faced the Etruscans, who were by this time too awed to hurl a single spear, and only began when Horatius jeered at them, calling them slaves of a king too haughty to fight. At last the spears came, but Horatius caught them on his shield, and stood his ground. Enraged, the Etruscans charged. But at that instant the bridge crashed. Amid the cheers of the Romans, Horatius leaped clear and swam the Tiber to safety.

The lack of a bridge did not long delay the Etruscans. They commandeered boats and sent detachments across the Tiber to ravage the fields and cut off the city's food supply. Just in time the Romans drove in their flocks, closed their gates, and reinforced their defenses. As the blockade tightened with the entire Etruscan army drawing closer and closer, the Romans decided to try a stratagem. Certain men were selected to drive the flocks out through the Esquiline gate, while fighting-men slipped out through another gate some distance away, where the enemy was unlikely to observe them.

The Etruscans rushed to secure the sheep. But the Romans were ready. They fell upon the unsuspecting enemy, who, retreating in haste, were attacked in the rear by the legions who had marched out from the other gate. Caught in a squeeze, few of the Etruscans escaped. The survivors, including Porsenna, reached their boats and escaped to Janiculum. This was the last time the Etruscans roamed so far afield.

The Romans wanted peace, though not by paying the price Tarquin demanded: his return to power. Matters were in this state when a young Roman, Gaius Mucius, went alone to the Etruscan camp on the Janiculum Hill. The men were being paid off. Without being observed, Gaius joined the line. At a table near the altar Porsenna and a secretary were seated, handing each man his pay. Gaius had never seen Porsenna, and since the two men at the table were dressed almost alike, he had no way of knowing which was the king. When he saw that most of the soldiers addressed themselves to one and seemed to ignore the other, he pressed closer to the table. Suddenly his dagger flashed out, and the secretary fell back dead.

Gaius was seized, as he expected to be. When questioned, he said boldly that Porsenna might kill him if he wished, but that in Rome other young men had sworn to assassinate him. One by one they would come. All were as fearless and as dedicated as he. To prove the truth of his words, Gaius thrust his right hand into the altar fire and held it there without flinching.

Unable to endure the sight of the burning hand, Porsenna leaped from his seat and ordered his guards to remove Gaius from the altar. "Go free, young man," he said, "you have dared to harm yourself more than me."

Gaius, not to be outdone in courtesy, then told Porsenna that three hundred young men had sworn to kill him.

"I drew the first lot," he added, "after me, the others will come, as they have sworn, one by one."

Porsenna, convinced that Gaius was telling the truth, sent him back to Rome with an offer of peace. His terms were threefold:

first, that Tarquin should regain his throne; second, the Veientes should have their lands restored; third, the garrison on the Janiculum Hill would only be withdrawn if the Romans sent hostages. The Romans refused to restore Tarquin, but they accepted the other two terms. When Porsenna withdrew from the fort on the Janiculum Hill, he left behind him a fully stocked camp for the citizens of Rome, presumably because he admired them for preferring starvation to foreign domination.

It is pleasant to hear, that in this period of struggle and turmoil heroism was not confined to the male sex. Among the hostages Porsenna demanded from Rome before he left his fort on the Janiculum Hill, was a young girl, Cloelia. The Etruscans, after abandoning the Hill, had encamped on their side of the Tiber. Cloelia managed to elude the guards and, with the other girls who were also hostages, swam the Tiber under a rain of arrows, and returned to Rome. Porsenna, torn between rage and admiration, said he cared nothing about the other girls, though if they were not returned he would consider the treaty broken, but that he must have the girl Cloelia, and that he would return her safe and inviolate.

Both sides kept the treaty. To honor Cloelia for her bravery, Porsenna told her she could take back with her half the hostages, and that she herself should choose them. When all were brought before her, Cloelia chose the young boys of the group and took them home with her.

Livy says that when peace was established the Romans honored Cloelia by memorializing her in an equestrian statue erected on the Sacred Way.

Tarquin had not yet given up hope. The following year he persuaded Porsenna to send an embassy to Rome, to ask whether, now that he was an old man, he might be permitted to return to the city for which he had done so much. When the request was refused, Tarquin left Cerveteri and went to Tusculum, only fifteen miles from Rome, where his daughter and his Latin son-in-law, Mamilius Octavius, were living.

It is not likely that under these circumstances Tarquin would have gone to Tusculum merely to visit his daughter; he must have known that a new revolt of the Latin people was brewing, and that his son-in-law was the leader of the thirty cities who were conspiring against Rome. In this revolt Tarquin would have seen a fresh opportunity for himself. For though more than ten years had already passed since he had lost his throne and every attempt to regain it had proved abortive, Tarquin clung to his hope. Obviously he had no inkling of the steady policy of aggrandisement Rome was pursuing, which only an avalanche could have halted. That avalanche the northern snows were already preparing.

The sixth century B.C., that brilliant century of Etruscan greatness, had passed into the fifth when Mamilius Octavius led the Latin cities to war. Rome met the challenge by appointing, for the first time, a dictator. Against his decisions there could be no appeal. The Sabines, who had previously revolted, were so appalled by this new evidence of Rome's determination to mow down all opposition that they humbly begged forgiveness. But when Rome demanded an exorbitant sum to pay for the damage they had inflicted, the Sabines refused.

At Lake Regillus near Tusculum the Latins and the Romans met. Both Tarquin and his son Titus went with Mamilius. This time Tarquin did not accompany the foot soldiers. Both he and his son rode on horseback, well-armed with sword and spear. As the two sides advanced toward each other, Tarquin caught sight of the Roman dictator; he was in the front line exhorting his men.

Forgetting his age, forgetting everything except his desire for revenge, Tarquin spurred his horse straight at the hated Roman. The two met full tilt, and Tarquin fell with a spear in his side. Titus was engaged on the other wing, but some of Tarquin's friends rushed up and rescued the old man.

On the other wing Mamilius and Titus were in trouble; Mamilius, wounded, had moved back to the second line, where he continued to direct the fighting. To stem a retreat, he ordered Titus with a cohort of mounted Etruscan exiles into the front line. So furious was the exiles' attack that the Roman line fell back in disorder. Just then a youthful horse commander recognized Titus and headed for him, his spear leveled for the thrust. Titus swerved. The Roman plunged blindly; too late he saw another exile hurl his spear. It passed through the young man's body and he crashed to the ground.

The Etruscan exiles pressed their advantage. Seeing the Roman front line give before the Etruscans, the wounded dictator ordered his men to dismount and fight on foot. The Latins and the Etruscans were forced back, step by step, until the last survivors reached their camp—and were cut to pieces.

Tarquin's son-in-law, Mamilius Octavius, and his son, Titus, were dead. We hear nothing of his widowed daughter at Tusculum, nothing of Tullia at Cerveteri. Tarquin himself appears at the court of Aristodemus, the King of Cumae, at whose hands he had received his first defeat in war. Aristodemus welcomed his former enemy and offered him asylum.

In 495 B.C. an announcement was made in Rome. Tarquin the Proud was dead. He had left a will in which, though his property in Rome no longer belonged to him, he had bequeathed it to Aristodemus.

Etruria received the news of Tarquin's death as a prediction of an evil, long withstood, but now looming closer. At the Sacred Grove, men whispered that Tinia had consulted the shrouded gods and had gained permission to hurl the first of his red thunderbolts; it had fallen upon the last of the three Etruscan kings of Rome. And no common man knew, in his despair, how or where the second bolt would strike, for upon these points Tages, the scion of Tinia, had not instructed even the *haruspices* of Tarquinia.

XVIII

Veii Loses Her Crown

"Veii, thou hadst a royal crown of old,
And in thy forum stood a throne of gold!"

These lines the Roman poet Propertius wrote about the beautiful hill city of Veii which long before his day had perished suddenly and utterly from the face of the earth. Now from its ashes, the poet adds, the summer corn grows. Propertius may have been drawn to write these lines by the sight of the royal armor of Lars Tolumnius, the *lucumo* of Veii, that still hung, as late as the time of the Emperor Augustus, in the temple of Jupiter Feretrius in Rome.

Livy, too, may have been inspired by the sight of that royal armor which the *lucumo* of Veii once wore, for he pictures him in glowing terms as he flashes across the field to do battle with the Romans, his horsemen galloping hard behind. The ambiguous expression Lars Tolumnius had tossed off while engaged in a game of dice had had serious consequences. Since the death of the Roman ambassadors was an infringement of international law, it provided Rome with grounds for attacking Fidenae in earnest, rather than merely embarking upon a punitive expedition to recapture a lost colony. Veii would necessarily be drawn into the conflict.

The dreaded Roman legions were dispatched to Fidenae. Cornelius Cossus, a Roman consul, led them. From Veii came the intrepid Lars Tolumnius with his horsemen. The two opposing forces met on the left bank of the Tiber, below the walls of Fidenae. Early in the battle, the two leaders came face to face, and the Roman with a single stroke of his sword struck off his opponent's head, pierced it with his spear, and carrying his trophy high in the air, crashed through the ranks of the horrified Veientes, shouting that he had avenged the murder of Rome's ambassadors. Thereafter, until the next emergency arose, Veii was governed, as was Rome after the expulsion of the Tarquins, by consuls elected to serve one year.

Veii's throne of gold may not have been entirely a feat of poetic imagination; the city on the right bank of the Tiber was renowned for her wealth, her luxurious mode of life, and her artistic ability. She has the distinction of having been the home of Vulca, the only outstanding Etruscan sculptor whose name has come down to us, and to whose school the famous life-sized Apollo is attributed.

The Apollo, (made of terra-cotta and painted in the archaic style), was discovered in 1916, when preliminary excavations were being made on a site where some archaeologists believed they might find traces of ancient Veii. They were elated when they discovered the foundations of a temple with a pool of water near by, since literary sources had spoken of a temple of Apollo in a sacred enclosure, where pilgrims came to seek relief from their ills in the healing waters of a pool.

As the excavations progressed, fragments of other painted terra-cotta statues were discovered. They had formed part of the decoration of the temple, and must have been thrown carelessly to the ground when the temple suffered in the general destruction of Veii. Fortunately, the Apollo is almost complete. Now one of the treasures of the Villa Giulia in Rome, the Apollo has been pronounced an Etruscan work of the late sixth or early fifth century B.C. when Veii was in her prime.

The struggle between Veii and Rome had, of course, begun long before Lars Tolumnius lost his life, trying to save Fidenae. During the fourteen wars Livy reports were fought in that small area of only nine miles between Veii and Rome, Fidenae had always sided with Veii in the centuries-old struggle over the control of the salt-works and the "salt-road" that led north to Veii and beyond.

Regardless of which city controlled the salt-works, the revenues always accrued to the government, either of Veii or of Rome. (In Italy salt is still a government monopoly.) The management of the salt-works must have fallen into the category of political favors that lay in the power of the chief of state to confer. Tarquin the Elder, we recall, after he gained control of Rome, appeased certain plebeians by offering them the opportunity to gain prestige and wealth by superintending the salt-works. Whether Tarquin's successors continued the practice history does not seem to have recorded. The chances are that the superintendency remained a political plum.

The expulsion of the Tarquins from Rome did not solve the problem of ownership of the salt-works, nor did the struggle between the two cities cease. Again and again the Seven Villages Veii had established at the mouth of the Tiber were raided, and the "salt-road" blocked.

Veii needed the salt-road; she also needed the Tiber, her only access to the Tyrrhenian Sea; she could not have her life-line cut and survive. Neither could Rome; her population was increasing and her fertile lands insufficient for her needs; she had to have more land to grow more grain and she had to bring it down the Tiber. Compromise was imperative, yet impossible to achieve.

Released from the yoke she had borne so long and so impatiently under her Etruscan kings, Rome had set about preparing yokes for others. Her first battle, at Lake Regillus in 496 B.C. had established her as the virtual head of the Latin League. Unlike the Etruscan Confederations which, loosely organized, were held together only by ties of religion, the Latin League was chiefly a military alliance. Its soldiers were equipped with iron-tipped spears, and this innovation gave them an almost incalculable advantage over the Etruscans, who clung stubbornly to the older spear with its softer bronze tip.

Tarquin the Proud, in his enforced exile, had discovered to his chagrin that the Etruscans would not or could not realize that the welfare of an individual city was the concern of all. Chiusi, it is true, had supported Porsenna, and other cities had supported their leaders, but these were private wars in which national pride had no part. No Etruscan city, until Veii swallowed her pride, had ever appealed to the Union of Rasenna; no attempt had ever been made to weld into a nation the independent city-states, nor to bring together into one current the two separate streams of Etruscan life. Rome, on the other hand, was growing strong externally and internally; pride of country was dawning, and an overriding ambition to become Mistress of the World.

Unaware that the expulsion of the Tarquins and the consequent loss of Rome marked the height of her supremacy and that from then on the whole of Etruria would be engaged in a losing struggle for survival, Veii kept a strangle-hold upon her rival's throat. From 485 to 474 B.C. she kept up the unequal struggle. Finally, to her humiliation, Veii agreed to a forty-year truce which obliged her to send grain and money to Rome. The salt-works became Roman.

During the interval between Tarquin's death early in the fifth century and the forty-year truce, Rome had been almost constantly at war. Harassed abroad by her enemies, she was also subjected to the embarrassment of a social revolution at home: the plebeians against the patricians. The fall of the monarchy had been a blow to the plebeians, for the kings, in need of their support against the patricians, had granted rights to them they now felt endangered.

Unfortunately for her hostile neighbors, especially the Etruscans, Rome's social unrest did not interfere with the prosecution of her wars, not until the plebeians in a body deserted the city and took refuge upon the Sacred Mount three miles away across the Anio River. Here they stayed until a compromise, including the right of political representation, brought them down. The Etruscan cities were affected because they too had the same problems, ruled as they were by their patrician *lucumones*.

The patricians of Vulci, hearing of Rome's difficulties, and remembering they had not been called to account for aiding the Latins in their effort to restore Tarquin, decided to seize the opportunity to launch an attack. In the midst of their preparations, a Roman force descended upon the city and carried off three hundred children as hostages. But when Vulci sent messengers to the Latins to ask for help, they refused; the disaster they had suffered at Lake Regillus made them not only unwilling to join Vulci but led them to seize the messengers and deliver them to Rome. In return the Senate released six thousand Latin captives and so earned the gratitude of one of Rome's most defiant enemies.

Almost immediately after this generous act, the ulcer, as one angry Roman Senator dubbed the city's plebeians, became more inflamed. Rome had no debtor's prison; instead, a plebeian who borrowed money from a patrician and was unable to pay his debt was bound over to his creditor and became a virtual slave, even to living in his house and working for him without pay. This happened frequently to returned soldiers. Resentment burst out when a certain man, who had distinguished himself in battle, escaped from his creditor's torture-chamber and publicly displayed his scourged back in the Forum.

The crowd who had gathered listened in mounting rage. While the sufferer had been fighting the Sabines his cottage had been burned and his flocks driven off. His taxes then came at the wrong moment, he contracted debts, his interest mounted, his farm was seized, and he himself carried off. The man's story flew from mouth to mouth. Soon throngs of debtors, some in chains, arrived, and rioting spread through the Forum. Senators had to be rescued from the mob and escorted to the Senate House, where they tried to find a way out of their dilemma.

In the midst of the general uproar some Latin horsemen galloped up shouting that a Volscian army was approaching. The plebeians were jubilant. Let the Senators do the fighting, they shouted, it was none of their affair. A consul dashed out of the Senate House and tried to calm the crowd. Finally he made a solemn promise, that henceforth no soldier's property should be seized while he was in camp, nor should any Roman citizen be held by a creditor and so prevented from fighting for his country. Reassured, the debtors took the military oath and prepared for war.

For the time being, the plebeians had gained their point, but the Etruscans had lost, for the debtors fought so courageously that the men of Vulci were defeated, and Rome refused to give up the three hundred child hostages. The plebeians soon lost the point they had gained, and when war with the Sabines broke out, not a man enlisted. Instead, secret meetings were held, and daily the ulcer grew. Some plebeians slipped out through the gates and went to join the Etruscans, who were beginning to hope that at last Rome would be brought low.

The hopes of the insurgent cities and of the plebeians were soon dashed, for the Senate appointed a dictator with full power; the plebeians marched out, gained a victory, and marched back, only to find upon their return that they were as badly off as before. The dictator resigned, saying he would not be a party to broken promises. The next time the consuls attempted to lead the plebeian legions out, they rebelled and in large numbers abandoned the city, which they said no longer belonged to them, but to the patricians.

The city was swept by panic; the plebeians who had stayed behind feared what the patricians might do, and the patricians feared the plebeians. All activities came to a standstill. At last the defenseless city sent to the recalcitrants a certain Agrippa noted for his reasonable approach to problems. He told the dissident plebeians a story.

Long ago the various members of man's body conspired against the belly, which did nothing except enjoy the good things brought to it; the hands would therefore no longer bring food to the

187

mouth; the mouth would accept nothing, nor would the teeth grind anything. While trying to starve the body, the members became weak. That the belly had its own task to perform became clear, since what it received it divided among the several parts, being especially mindful of the blood by which the whole man is nourished.

Agrippa arranged a compromise: the plebeians were to choose two magistrates, to be called "tribunes of the people." The persons of these tribunes were to be inviolable; any one who touched them would be under a curse. This time the plebeians had really gained a point.

The following year, though, the price of grain went up, and for this the plebeians were blamed, because during their absence on the Sacred Mount the fields had been neglected, and grain was now so scarce that Rome was threatened with a famine. The consuls bought up grain wherever they could find it. (In Cumae Aristodemus seized the grain ships, to punish Rome for not having delivered Tarquin's property that had been bequeathed to him.) At Rome, when the grain arrived, much of it from Sicily, some of the patricians wanted to charge the plebeians higher prices; fortunately, cooler heads prevailed.

Throughout Etruria, during the following years, the course of events at Rome was closely watched, in the hope that civil discord would effect her downfall. And it did seem that this could not long be put off, for in 480 B.C. the Roman soldiers disobeyed their commanders in the field, deserted their standards, and returned without orders to their camp. This was the year when the Athenian democracy defeated the Persian king at Salamis.

Now at last fate seemed to have put the cards into Etruscan hands; a show of arms would surely topple the Roman camp. Boldly the Veientes and their allies rode up to the camp and challenged the Romans to come out and fight. Afraid to trust their soldiers, the commanders disregarded the challenge. The Etruscans hurled insults, but they did not attack the camp. Historians have always wondered why. Some think the Etruscans were too confident, believing that if they continued to jeer, the Roman soldiers would lay down their arms. Instead, they began to clamor, vowing they would fight to the death. The camp gates were thrown open; the Etruscans were caught off guard, aimed their spears badly, and were obliged to fight at swords' point. Finally, though at tremendous cost, the Romans won.

During the following year, Livy states, there was neither peace nor war; the Etruscans raided the Roman fields, destroying crops, carrying off booty, keeping the countryside in constant terror. Rome seemed afflicted with the palsy. In 478 B.C. the Veientes took advantage of Rome's preoccupation with other rebelling peoples to march directly upon the city. Then occurred an instance of patriotic devotion that has seldom been equalled.

The men of an entire Roman clan, the Fabii, asked permission of the Senate to take the field against the Etruscans. "Leave the Etruscans to us," the consul Caeso Fabius said to the Senate. "Do you engage our other enemies."

The next morning Caeso Fabius led forth his clan, all of patrician blood, three hundred and six, sworn to destroy the Veientes or die on the field. Filled with admiration, the whole city accompanied the Fabii to the gates and watched them march away, banners tossing in the wind. At the Cremara River the Fabii built a fort. There they remained, and for a while the Etruscans ceased their raids, such havoc did the Fabii wreak.

In 477 B.C. the Veientes devised a plan. They drove flocks among the Fabii and then fled in pretended terror from their pursuers. The Fabii, emboldened by frequent successes, rushed to secure the animals and fell into an ambush. Of the three hundred and six patricians who had marched out from Rome, only one, a boy, survived.

Again the Veientes did not take advantage of their success. If they had besieged Rome, the whole course of Mediterranean history might have been changed. Instead they took possession of the Janiculum Hill, where they held out for many months until they were dislodged and cut down as they fled. And so in 475 B.C. the

Veientes sued for their forty-year peace. But no sooner was the truce ended than the rivals were again at each other's throats. This was the eleventh war. In the twelfth, Lars Tolumnius was killed and Fidenae lost. Another truce was agreed upon, this time for twenty years.

Veii, who had "of old" worn her "royal crown" so proudly and whose fighting-men had seized the Janiculum Hill, Veii, the Troy of Italy, the bulwark of southern Etruria, seems to have felt, when war again broke out after the twenty-year truce, that her end was in sight. The Tagetic Doctrine had inculcated in her leaders, as among other Etruscans, the belief that all events were ordained and that there was no final escape. Therefore, when in 406 B.C. the war started again, Veii gathered herself together and prepared for her trial. After ten years of harassment, her trial became an ordeal by fire.

About the ninth year, when the struggle appeared deadlocked, strange and mysterious portents were whispered of, and in both Veii and Rome people became alarmed. Livy reports that no soothsayers were able to interpret the omens. At last, unaccountably, the level of the Alban Lake near Rome began to rise. Terrified, the Romans dispatched messengers to Delphi to seek advice. Before the messengers returned, the Romans learned what the overflowing of the lake meant. One day the Roman and the Veientian guards at the city wall were, as usual, fraternizing with one another, exchanging quips and jests, when one of the Romans overheard an Etruscan voice chanting that Veii could never be captured until the lake was drained. Upon inquiry, the Roman learned that the voice was that of an Etruscan seer. Pretending to need counsel, the Roman guard managed to meet the seer and Plutarch reports snatch him up by the middle. Dragged into the Roman camp, and taken from there before the Roman Senate, the Etruscan was commanded to explain his chanted words.

"In our books of destiny," the prisoner explained, "it has been recorded that, if any one were to drain off in the correct manner the overflow of the Alban Lake, Veii could be captured."

The seer, under pressure, then haltingly explained how the lake should be drained. The Senate, doubting the seer's word, waited for the messengers to return from Delphi. Their report confirmed the seer's explanation. Interpreted, the advice from Delphi became clear; the Romans must irrigate their own lands before trying to take the lands of another people.

Von Vacano's explanation of this apparent betrayal by the Etruscan of his own countrymen is that the seer's dilemma is comparable to that of a person with the "terrible gift" of second sight who dreads to make known his vision, yet fears the consequences of his failure to do so.

The tenth year of this "Trojan war" arrived. But it was not in the belly of a wooden horse that the enemy entered Veii; it was through a carefully-prepared tunnel. Marcus Furius Camillus, who had been given dictatorial power, led the Roman forces; in 396 B.C., despairing of taking Veii by assault, he tried stratagem. He bored a tunnel up through the soft tufa until he reached the floor of a temple dedicated to the goddess Uni. Then with trusted men at his back he entered the tunnel on a day when sacrifices were being offered.

"Whoever places these entrails upon the altar shall have the victory," came to the ears of Camillus and his men concealed in the tunnel below.

With a muttered signal to his men, Camillus burst out through the floor, seized the entrails, and made the offering on the altar. Now Camillus had vowed that, if the gods permitted him to capture Veii he would offer a tenth of his booty to the oracle at Delphi, institute games at Rome and erect a temple to the goddess Uni on the Aventine Hill, provided the goddess consented to leave her city. Livy describes the ceremony.

The best-formed youths of the army were selected. They were bathed, anointed, dressed in fresh white robes, and led to the temple of Uni. There they laid hands on the goddess, who never before had been touched by any hand except that of her own attendant priest, and reverently lifted her down from her pedestal, first having asked her consent. It is related that in an audible voice she consented.

Camillus kept his vow. He sent a tenth of his booty to Delphi, instituted games at Rome, and four years after the fall of Veii the goddess Uni was installed in a temple on the Aventine Hill.

Reports about the destruction of Veii do not agree. The usual story is that when the gates of the city had closed behind the departing goddess, terror took her place. Men who survived the battle were slain, women and children were sold into slavery, and the city was destroyed.

Veii could not have been completely destroyed, for at Rome it was proposed that the plebeians should be sent there to live. Rome would then become a patrician city. Nothing came of this proposal. Nine years later, when Rome was sacked by the Gauls, many patricians fled to Veii.

Camillus is said to have wept when he looked upon the ruins of Veii, for generations so secure upon her hill top that her population had grown to one hundred thousand souls. Of these only a handful had survived the holocaust and remained free; and Camillus vowed not to seek them out. At last Veii's stubborn resistance to Rome's onward march had been overcome. Still, if the Union of Rasenna had not been so apathetic, so blind to the danger that threatened all Etruria if their southern rampart should fall, Veii might have been saved.

Perugia was also a hill town. She too belonged to the confederation, along with Arezzo and Cortona, her nearest neighbors, for whom she would form a strong rampart, if ever Rome started northward. This the whole confederation must have realized, but we have no information that it ever sent help to Perugia when in 308 B.C. her first trial came, any more than it did to Veii.

For three hundred years the empty houses and the silent streets of Veii were left to decay. Then the Emperor Augustus established a small colony within its broken walls. The attempt did not succeed: the colony gradually and mysteriously disappeared. The people may have succumbed to the insidious malaria that rose up from the long-neglected swamps which the Etruscans had known how to drain.

Soon beautiful Veii was no more; she had lost the focus of her life, the jewel in her royal crown, the goddess Uni, who under the guise of the Roman Juno dwelt in her new temple on the Aventine Hill.

To many throughout Etruria it must have seemed that the great god Tinia had hurled his second red thunderbolt.

XIX

Perugia Falls to Rome

Unaware of the avalanche that was fast thundering down upon her from the far north, Rome continued, after her conquest of Veii, to attack small nearby Etruscan cities, helpless now without Veii to protect them. Since captured cities were required to pay the expenses of successful campaigns against them, during these years Rome could afford to exempt her citizens from the customary war tax.

While Rome was busily engaged in extending her power over central Etruria, one day a certain plebeian told his tribune that during the night he had heard a voice bidding him warn the city that Gauls had appeared in the north.

"This portent was neglected, as often happens," Livy reports, "because of the informant's humble station."

Not long afterward, rumors flew from mouth to mouth, thick and fast, that hordes of shaggy Gauls had erupted from their forests and were pouring into the Po valley. Before these savages, with long reddish hair and frightening blue eyes, yelling in a rough, uncouth tongue, the Etruscans in the north had fled in terror.

The Roman historian, Cornelius Nepos, reports that on the same day that Veii fell, the Gauls had captured and sacked the wealthy

Etruscan city of Melpum on the Po River (near the present site of Milan). Driven by the need of more living-space than their homeland beyond the Alps could supply for their increasingly large population, the Gauls had uprooted themselves and started southward. Led by their chief, Brennus (his historical existence is doubtful), and attracted by tales of luscious fruit and choice wines, the Gauls pressed on wave after wave into Central Etruria, the land of plenty where gold and silver and all good things were to be had for the plucking. Their raids spread such terror that in 390 or 387 B.C. they had arrived with little opposition at the gates of Rome.

Adventurers rather than conquerors, at first the Gauls contented themselves with seizing Etruscan lands and settling their families. Soon their presence became a source of constant danger to the Etruscan cities, especially to Chiusi on the inland road to central Etruria, and men feared they would be caught between the Gauls to the north and the Romans to the south.

When the Gauls struck, they attacked Chiusi first, down whose hill Porsenna with his men of bronze had clattered in a vain attempt to reseat Tarquin the Proud upon his throne and make Rome once again an Etruscan city controlled by the laws of Tages. Chiusi, in dire peril and remembering that Veii had appealed in vain for assistance from the Union of Rasenna that met in the sacred Grove, was not willing to subject herself to such humiliation. There is no record that she turned to the northern confederation or even that the confederation was still in existence. Instead, then, of calling upon any of the Etruscan cities for assistance, Chiusi turned to Rome.

Some historians think this turning to Rome at such a critical point in the long struggle between the Etruscans and the Romans means that no national enmity could really have existed, otherwise Chiusi would not have asked aid of Rome, nor would Rome have tried to arbitrate between the Gauls and Chiusi. Perhaps Rome thought the Gauls a greater threat than the Etruscans. If so, then her intervention was in her own interests.

The negotiators whom Rome sent to Chiusi were unsuccessful, since neither disputant would yield to the other. Out of patience, the negotiators made a mistake; they broke the sacred law which forbade emissaries to take sides, and advised Chiusi to stand firm. Infuriated by this breach, the Gauls bypassed Chiusi and advanced upon Rome, ignoring the Etruscan settlements between the two cities. But the Etruscans were not so easily ignored. Though hampered by their bronze armor and unable to move fast enough to out-maneuver the more lightly-armed Gauls, the Etruscans opposed the wild hordes wherever they could.

The Roman Senate, fearful that their sacred hearth-fire might be desecrated, ordered the Vestal Virgins to gather up all the holy things and take them to Cerveteri. Unable to carry everything, the Vestals hid some in jars and buried them in a shrine. Legend adds that since then it has been forbidden to any person to spit near the shrine.

Loaded down with what they could carry, the Vestals crossed the Sublician Bridge and started up the Janiculum Hill. Among the refugees who were fleeing from Rome was a plebeian who was walking beside a cart in which his wife and children rode. As soon as he saw the Vestals, he bade his wife and children dismount, placed the holy women and their sacred things in the cart, and brought them safely to Cerveteri.

Stunned by the swiftness of the Gauls and knowing that most of the Roman legions were away fighting the Etruscans, the tribunes hastily mustered their reserves and met the Gauls near the Tiber. Out-manned, out-generalled, and completely unnerved by the wild Gallic yells and songs, the Romans broke. Soon the whole plain was dotted with armor and weapons, over which pursued and pursuers stumbled and fell. Hundreds of fleeing Romans took refuge in Veii.

Since those who succeeded in getting into Veii sent no reassurance to Rome, the legions, thinking they alone had escaped the Gauls, rushed pell-mell through the gates, so terrified that they did not stop to close them in their mad race for the Capitoline Hill.

The Gauls, amazed by their victory, marched on Rome. There they were more amazed to find the gates open, the walls unguarded, and the air filled with sounds of weeping. Suspecting an ambush, they passed the night outside, feasting and singing. Inside the city the young and strong were sent to hold the Capitoline Hill, all others were ordered to take shelter where they could.

At dawn the Gauls marched through the open gates into what appeared to be a deserted city. They roamed about in search of booty; they entered closed houses and found them empty (these were plebeian houses, Livy tells us, whose occupants were on their way to the Janiculum Hill); finally some of them wandered into open mansions where they "beheld seated in the vestibules, beings who, besides that their ornaments and apparel were more splendid than belonged to man, seemed also, in their majesty of countenance and in the gravity of their expression, most like to gods."

The Gauls did not know they were looking at elderly patricians who had once held high office. Now too old to fight, they had put on their magisterial robes and seated themselves in their ivory chairs to await death. They had not long to wait, for when a Gallic hand softly touched the long beard of one of the statuesque beings, the image came instantly to life and with an ivory staff struck the Gaul over the head. In the massacre that followed none of the nobles escaped. Nor was any mercy shown to people caught in the streets or in their houses, which were then pillaged and fired.

The defenders on the Capitoline Hill could scarcely be restrained from rushing down, as day after day they heard the cries of the people, the crackling of the flames, and the crash of falling timbers. One wonders what the Romans thought, now that they were experiencing for the first time what they had so often inflicted upon the Etruscans.

Day and night the carnage went on. Finally the Gauls advanced on the Capitoline Hill. Holding their shields overhead, they began to climb the rocky, precipitous hill. The Romans met them halfway, dislodged the first Gaul in the line, and hurled him, a human catapult, down upon his fellows. Man after man lost his foothold and landed in a heap of flailing arms and legs at the bottom of the hill.

Unable to take the hill by assault, the Gauls decided upon a blockade. But since their fires had destroyed all the stored grain, and the crops outside had been taken to Veii, they were faced with a famine and had to divide their army, half to forage for food and wine, half to set up the blockade.

The foraging army arrived at Ardea, where Tarquin's son Sextus had been murdered. In Ardea, Camillus, the conqueror of Veii, was living in exile. Hearing that the Senate was deliberating how to meet the Gauls, he offered to lead the men of Ardea in a night attack. The Gauls, he told the Senate, seldom made camp at night; they would be found sleeping here and there on the ground and could easily be butchered.

The Senate accepted the offer; Camillus and his men descended upon the sleeping Gauls, killed all who could not escape, and returned triumphantly to Ardea.

Meanwhile, at Veii men were assembling from every quarter, determined to drive the savage Gauls out of the country. Some one proposed to send for Camillus. But for an exile to conduct a campaign permission had to be secured from Rome. Supported on a piece of cork, a young man floated down the Tiber, climbed up the steepest side of the Capitoline Hill, and delivered the request. At a hasty meeting the Senators rescinded the decree of exile and appointed Camillus dictator.

The Gauls soon discovered the messenger's tracks. On a starlit night, they again tried to climb the Capitoline Hill. They pulled each other up and reached the unguarded summit without arousing even the dogs. Unfortunately for the invaders, they knew nothing about Juno's sacred geese. The creatures flapped their wings and gabbled so noisily that they awakened a Roman officer who sprang up and rushed to the edge of the precipice, arriving just in time to see a helmeted head appear. Instantly the

Roman struck. As the Gaul slipped and fell, he overturned the men behind him and, as on the earlier occasion, the whole line of climbers landed in a heap at the foot of the hill, providing an excellent target for the javelins of the rest of the defenders who had hurried to the crest of the hill.

The second attempt having failed, the Gauls vented their anger on the people who had previously escaped them. So many bodies were left unburied in the streets that a plague broke out, from which many Romans and Gauls died. Both sides were now eager for a truce. The Gauls demanded a thousand pounds of gold. The transaction was well under way, when the Roman leader, seeing that false weights were being used, called a halt.

"*Vae victis*" (woe to the vanquished) shouted Brennus, and added his sword to the weight.

Just then Camillus arrived—he had been out building up a fresh fighting force—with a legion at his back. Scornfully he informed Brennus that Rome would not buy her freedom with gold, but with iron. The Gauls instantly attacked the Romans; driven back to a distance of eight miles, the Gauls rallied and fought. But fortune was now with the Romans, for not a single Gaul survived that battle.

In 310 B.C. some eighty years after the Gauls had been defeated, the Romans, anxious to extend their conquests beyond central Etruria, decided to send an expedition into the mountainous country to the northeast near Perugia, where even itinerant traders had never dared venture. The Roman consul, Quintus Fabius, was placed in charge. To secure information about the trackless forest the army would have to penetrate, the consul's brother Marcus, who, as Livy relates, had been educated in Cerveteri and knew the Etruscan language, disguised himself as a shepherd and, with his trusted slave who had been educated with him, went through the dark, almost impenetrable forest and finally reached Chiusi, where they revealed their identity.

Impressed by the daring of the two young men, Chiusi promised to support an army for a month if it actually succeeded in getting through the forest, as no one expected it to be able to do. With his brother's information to aid him, Quintus Fabius and his army slipped through the mountains during the night and at dawn, not trusting the offer from Chiusi, attacked the small knots of peasants the surprised nobles had hastily assembled. Other nobility of the region joined Chiusi. Out-numbered and out-flanked, thousands fell or were taken prisoner by the Romans. Three neighboring cities, Perugia, Cortona, and Arezzo, all close to the foot hills of the Apennines, sued for peace and an alliance with Rome.

In the face of Rome's increasing hostility, the Etruscans and the Gauls now banded together for mutual protection. In 308 B.C. a "sacred law" was passed, which Livy explains as a "law promulgated in the name of the gods," intended to revive an ancient recruiting system completely unlike the Roman conscription of citizens or even the earlier tribal organization where each man owed allegiance to his chief. The sacred law required each noble to form an armed nucleus of his own friends. Then each member of the nucleus was to collect his friends and acquaintances, who were in their turn to collect a further group. The system created almost as many leaders as there were followers, and must have divided loyalties. But this was the old way, and to the Etruscans the old way was sacrosanct. More than one scholar has pointed out that such a system had the disadvantage of producing a private army and not a national one.

This privately-recruited Etruscan army engaged the Romans near Perugia, at Lake Vadimon, a small sulphur lake that had filled up the crater of an extinct volcano. The fighting was so severe and the casualties so great that the Roman cavalry dismounted and fought on foot over the heaped-up dead. Their intervention turned the tide of battle; the Etruscans broke ranks and fled in wild disorder. For the first time, Livy reports, the power of the Etruscans in the north was broken. Elated, Quintus Fabius pressed on toward his goal, the high-walled city of Perugia. The Perugians marched out to give battle. Swiftly the Romans disposed of them. The way open, the Roman forces soon appeared under the walls. Perugia surrendered in 308 B.C., and had to send ambassadors to plead for peace from the Roman Senate.

Five years later a Roman army marched northwestward and attacked Rusellae, a walled Etruscan town on the Ombrone River. This too was a private war and for the second time the military power of the Etruscans was broken.

After the first battle at Lake Vadimon, Tarquinia had asked and obtained from Rome a forty-year truce. Now with Rusellae conquered and no opposition from Tarquinia, Rome was free to attack the wealthy ore-bearing country of northwestern Etruria. Soon she had conquered the coastal cities of Vetulonia and Populonia, and Volterra inland from the coast.

Deprived of their supply of ore from Vetulonia, Populonia, and Volterra, which now provided the Romans with their war material, the Etruscans formed an alliance with a Gallic tribe that had set out on its own to conquer Rome. At Lake Vadimon, where fifteen years before the Etruscans had suffered a crushing defeat, with their new Gallic allies they engaged in a second desperate battle with the Romans. Once more the Romans defeated them, this time so severely that in the report that has come down to us the Tiber flowed crimson with Etruscan blood.

The internal dissensions between patricians and plebeians that had plagued Rome for many centuries were also rife in Etruria. Just when internal unity was of prime importance to combat enemy pressure, civil dissensions invariably broke out. One of the worst of these disasters occurred some twenty years after the Etruscan defeat at Rusellae, and caused the fall of Volsinia, in whose territory lay the sacred Grove of Voltumna.

In the year 280 B.C. the quarrel between the noble families of Volsinia and their slaves became acute. The bitter conflict with Rome had obliged the noblemen of Volsinia to arm their slaves and lead them into battle. To force these unwilling men to fight, the noblemen had promised them rights that had previously been denied: the right to a seat in the Senate, to vote, to inherit, and to marry into the patrician class. Plebeians may also have been under some, if not all, of these restrictions, as they were in Rome before Servius Tullius introduced his reforms.

Volsinia, aided by her neighbors, had put up a tough resistance to Rome, no doubt, as has been suggested, because the Etruscans feared to let the sacred Grove fall into Roman hands. Since the patricians everywhere in Etruria had had to bear the cost of war, their resources gradually diminished. In Volsinia the patricians, trying to avoid keeping their promises to grant rights to the slaves, appealed to Rome for aid in subduing the rebels.

The rebels learned of this treacherous attempt and, as patrician Rome had feared would happen when Servius Tullius armed the plebeians, the slaves turned on their former masters. They took control of the city, killed all the patricians they could catch, seized their widows, and changed the ancient "right of the first night," hitherto applicable only to lower class daughters, to include the daughters of patricians.

Rome intervened, blockaded Volsinia until hunger finally forced the rebels to surrender, and then executed them. The triumphant Romans moved out the survivors with their families, resettled them on the shore of Lake Bolsena, and destroyed Volsinia. This brought Etruria closer to economic collapse. Unification with Rome was not far distant.

Apparently Rome did not interfere with the sacred Grove, but some Etruscan inscriptions seem to indicate that Tarquinia now became the headquarters for training the soothsayers.

Rome's long drawn out conflict with Carthage, which lasted over a hundred years, brought the Etruscan cities, one by one, into her orbit as colonies. Instead of being proud city-states the Etruscan cities had become small provincial towns where the ruling families felt secure, and whatever revolts flared up were easily and quickly disposed of. That Rome's policy was bearing fruit in central Etruria was evident when the Gauls took advantage of her trouble with Carthage to launch a powerful invasion that swept everything before it. In earlier years this would have been the signal for the Etruscans to join the Gauls against Rome. Rome's terror was so great that when an oracle bade her sacrifice two human victims, she buried alive in the cattle market two Gauls, a man and a woman.

Nor was there an uprising when eight years later the Carthaginians under Hannibal inflicted a terrible defeat upon the Romans at Lake Trasimene near Perugia. When the war was pushed into Africa, some twelve years after the disaster at Trasimene, eight Etruscan cities, including Perugia, provided Rome with greatly needed supplies for carrying the war to a successful close.

In the first century B.C., the civil war between Sulla and Marius put the loyalty of many Etruscan cities to a severe test. As Roman citizens they could not remain neutral; they had to choose between Sulla and Marius, even though for them the choice was between Scylla and Charybdis. Arezzo, Cortona, Fiesole, Populonia, and Volterra chose Marius, the plebeian, unwisely for them, as the sequel proved, because victorious Sulla exacted a terrible revenge from the Etruscan families who had taken his rival's side. Few of them escaped. Then to form a new and mixed population, Sulla sent in to each city Roman colonists.

In 88 B.C. Sulla died, of a burst blood vessel. This date, according to the Etruscan chronology, marks the end of Etruria.

But the end was not yet come. Perugia continued to exist behind her great towering walls. Within the circuit of those walls dwelt a brave and patriotic man, Cestio, whom history has all but forgotten. Three years after the assassination of Julius Caesar in 44 B.C. Mark Antony's brother Lucius, fleeing from Octavian, the future Augustus, took refuge in Perugia where he had many supporters among the patricians. When Octavian besieged Perugia, famine forced the city to surrender. Octavian announced that he would pardon Antony and his supporters on one condition, that three hundred Senators be given up for execution.

Perugia surrendered its Senators. In the city, altars were set up, near one that had been erected in honor of Julius Caesar. Before these altars the three hundred Senators were slaughtered. Octavian then announced that he would order his men to pillage and burn the city.

Cestio, unable to brook this final insult to his beloved Perugia, forestalled the Roman torches. With his own hand, he set fire to his house, leaped into its flames, and perished.

Some modern writers have seen in the complete destruction the Romans visited upon the Etruscans all the elements of a Greek tragedy. Tanaquil herself, they feel, sowed the seeds of tragedy that day in 632 B.C., when she sat beside her Lucumo on the Janiculum Hill and, for ambition's sake, persuaded him to enter Rome under a new name. Or, the blame may rest upon great Tinia, who had already shot two of the three red thunderbolts at his disposal. One had slain Tarquin the Proud, the other had fallen upon Veii. Now, foreseeing it inevitable that he should follow Uni to Rome and become the Jupiter of the Romans, perchance he sympathized with Cestio and with his own divine hand hurled upon Perugia his third and last red thunderbolt.

XX

Time and Destiny

During the same year (1916) that the Apollo of Veii was discovered, an unusually large and handsome bronze mirror was found in the ruins of Perugia. Experts have dated this Athrpa mirror, as it is called from a name inscribed on its reverse, at approximately 320 B.C., some twelve years before the Romans first attacked Perugia.

The experts think that the Athrpa mirror, unfortunately no longer in Perugia but in Wiesbaden, Germany, was cast in one piece with its tongue, which was then enclosed in a haft of bone or wood that is now missing. No one seems to know whether the mirror was manufactured in Perugia or brought in from the outside. Its size is remarkable, the largest of almost two thousand mirrors in present-day museums; even without the original haft, its height is over twelve inches and its reflecting surface almost eight in diameter.

Neither the mirror from Vulci, in the Gregorian Museum of the Vatican, nor the Tarchon mirror, in the Archaeological Museum at Florence, could have offered the unknown engraver of the Athrpa mirror the necessary space for the scene he has portrayed with such clarity, a tragic episode of the Calydonian boar-hunt.

Those who trust the proverb, that coming events often cast their shadows before, will surely wonder why, at that particular moment in Etruscan history, an artist should engrave upon a mirror a scene that points so unmistakably to the finiteness of time and the part that destiny, blindly or not, plays in human affairs. Perhaps the engraver was unaware of the prophecy that set a precise end for the Etruscans as an ethnic entity, or he may have been merely carrying out a commission for some aristocratic lady who, in common with other Etruscan women of the fourth century b.c., sorrowed for the death of Adonis, who in the prime of his youthful beauty was gored to death on the horns of a boar.

The Greek legend of the Calydonian boar-hunt relates how Meleager, the king of Calydon, and Atalanta, the virgin huntress, met each other in the forest and fell in love. But since destiny had long since marked Meleager for her own, the course of their true love was turned aside and Meleager came to an untimely death.

The story runs that the youthful king of Calydon had invited the neighboring princes to join him in ridding their forest of a gigantic boar the Greek goddess Artemis, angered because of a sacrifice forgotten, had sent upon them.

The princes eagerly responded to Meleager's urgent call. Atalanta, who had disappointed her father by not being born a boy, also came. According to the custom of the day, the unwanted girl-child had been left out in the open to die. But a bear found her and nurtured her. When she grew up and returned to her parents, her father urged her to marry; she refused to wed any man except one who would race with her and be willing to die if he lost. Every school child knows how Atalanta was tricked into marriage by the hero who dropped the three golden apples which she picked up as she ran and so lost the race.

Among the heroes who responded to Meleager's call were his mother's two brothers. The hunt was going well when suddenly the boar sprang out of hiding and confronted Atalanta, who hurled her spear at him, and wounded but did not kill him. Before the maddened beast could turn upon Atalanta, Meleager rushed up and dispatched him with a second spear-thrust.

Instead of claiming the honor of the "first spear," Meleager presented the trophy of the chase—the boar's hide—to Atalanta. Angered by such conduct on their nephew's part, Meleager's uncles took the hide from Atalanta and gave it back to Meleager. In the quarrel that followed, Meleager killed his mother's brothers.

On the Athrpa mirror, to make sure that the object of the hunt will be understood, the engraver has placed a boar's head at the top of his design, which includes the principals in the hunt, Meleager and Atalanta, and three other figures. Above the heads of all except one their names are written in Etruscan characters. The scene represents the moment when realization of the blood-crime he has committed breaks in all its horror upon Meleager.

Atalanta, in Etruscan Atlenta, is portrayed as a beautiful young woman completely nude. The engraver has been unable to refrain from giving her a necklace and one bracelet. Seated on a stool, Atalanta holds in her hand the spear with which, according to the Greek myth, she has just wounded the boar. Meleager (Meliacr) also nude, stands beside her, his spear in his right hand, his left pointing down at the trophy that has caused the trouble. His face, far from expressing love for Atalanta or triumph for his own success, is as sad as hers.

On Meleager's other side stands a nude young woman with great sweeping wings. She wears bracelets and a magnificent necklace that looks as though it had come from an Egyptian lady's jewel-box. Over her head is written Athrpa. Von Vacano interprets Athrpa as the Etruscan counterpart of the Greek Atropos, one of the three weird sisters who control the whole of man's life. Of the three, Atropos, who is represented in Greek art and literature with a pair of shears in her hand, is the one who cuts the thread of a man's life when his time on earth has reached its end. But instead of a pair of shears the Etruscan Athrpa holds a hammer and a nail. For an Etruscan the act of driving in a nail had the same symbolic significance as the cutting of the thread had for a Greek; acceptance of the inevitability of divine fate.

Atalanta's face is turned away from Meleager and the trophy at her feet. Her attitude accentuates the spectator's conviction that every person in the scene knows what fate holds in store for Meleager. His gallantry in rescuing Atalanta by delivering the death-blow when he saw that she was in danger is not to be rewarded, since he has had the misfortune to slay his uncles. This was indeed a misfortune, because his mother's parents were dead, and she could never hope for other brothers to replace those she had lost. In her wild grief, she recalled a prophecy made at Meleager's birth, that the child's life was linked with a log then burning on the hearth. To preserve her son's life, she had snatched out the log, and concealed it in a chest. Meleager grew to young manhood, met Atalanta, and fell in love. But his mother, when she heard that her brothers were dead by the hand of her son, thought only of them. She ran to the chest, took out the charred log, and threw it into the fire. As the log burned, her son's life ebbed away.

Two figures in this interesting scene on the mirror are still to be accounted for, a female figure and a male. The composition of the scene is admirable and its balance flawless. The female figure—the partly defaced name over her head has been interpreted as that of Turan, the Etruscan Aphrodite—stands opposite that of Meleager, while the seated youth beside her balances the seated Atalanta. The youth is the beautiful Adonis over whom the Greek goddess of love, Aphrodite, quarreled with Persephone, the goddess of the underworld. The Greek myth relates that the two goddesses asked Zeus to decide which of them should possess the youth, still radiant in death. But Zeus had no power over Fate; he could only decree that the goddesses should take turns, six months at a time. Now when winter comes and the things of the earth wither and pass away, Adonis goes below to sleep his allotted six months in the arms of Persephone. With the spring flowers he returns, and finds his joy in the arms of Aphrodite.

The position the engraver has assigned to the goddess Athrpa makes clear the relationship between Adonis and Meleager: her right hand, holding the hammer of destiny, rests on Adonis; her upraised left hand hovers over Meleager's head. Both are doomed men. Aphrodite, who stands with her head bent slightly toward Adonis and one hand on his shoulder, knows how powerless she is; Atalanta looks away from Meleager as though she cannot bear to fact the truth she knows she must admit, if she looks into his eyes. The emphasis of the scene is not on reunion; it is on the sadness of separation.

Only a vegetation myth, we explain in our prosaic modern way, but who is to know whether winter's cold will ever lessen for either the spring flowers or for mortal man?

Contact with Hellenistic Greece probably brought the Adonis myth to Etruria. Once established, the myth became the focus of a woman's cult that gained strength from a belief to which the trembling hopes of all clung, that through prayers, sacrifices, and expiation ceremonies they too might gain a deferment of their fate. The door to the Lower World could not remain closed forever, they knew that; yet its opening might perhaps, just perhaps, be postponed. Then a little while longer they may enjoy the sunshine before they must pass through the door and face what lies beyond.

Urn-reliefs from Volterra sometimes show this mysterious door, often under an archway. From Volterra has also come the ash-urn with the worried-looking couple sculptured on its lid. For during the fourth century B.C. the Etruscan attitude toward life in the next world had begun to change. No longer, as in the past, does an expectant youth, whose career on earth is ended, stand erect and proud in his chariot, driving his spirited horses across the void to his new home. A kindly messenger escorts him; she carries in her hand a list of his deeds, good and bad, for which he will not be afraid to answer before the judge of all men. But by the fourth century he has begun to be afraid.

The change of attitude appears in a horrifying fresco from a tomb in Tarquinia. Here we have a foreboding of the mysterious world that awaits the dead in the Lower World. The artist has shown Tuchulcha, the demon of death, in the most bestial form imaginable, a taste of what awaits the dead. Tuchulcha's baleful eyes, grinning mouth, and vulture-like beak must have caused many an Etruscan nightmare. His horses are serpents, his hair writhes, and a monstrous serpent weaves near his head.

Faced with a future spent in Tuchulcha's company, it is no wonder that the Etruscans resorted to any means in their power to defer that last journey, if only for the doubtful pleasure of a few more years in a steadily shrinking land.

". . . the tragic view of the finiteness of life and love, and the subjection of gods and men to omnipotent fate"; writes von Vacano ". . . all these are features of the Greek world of tradition which would certainly move Etruscans when they looked at such pictures as that on the Athrpa mirror. . . the juxta-position of Atalanta-Meleager and Aphrodite-Adonis beneath the sign of the boar's head . . . grouped around Athrpa, standing ready to hammer home her nails."

Throughout the ancient world there seems to have been a feeling —some call it a theory—that mankind was in a process of gradual deterioration from a state of early blessedness to a state of wretched misery in which every man's hand would be raised against his neighbor's. This feeling is crystalized in the Boeotian poet Hesiod who lived in the eighth century B.C. and who included it in his epic poem, *Works and Days.* Here for the first time in literature we hear about the four metal ages of the world: gold, silver, bronze, and iron, and the manner of life in each age. At last, in the cruel age of iron, Justice forsakes the world and flees upward to rejoin the blessed gods, since in the world of man, as the poet cries, "There is naught which avails against evil."

Between the age of bronze, and the age of iron in which Hesiod complains that he is fated to live, he inserts the age of heroes, those splendid heroes of Homer's day whom he thinks of as demi-gods. Discarding the interpolated age, we are confronted with a belief which regards history as divided into four parts, each with a breed of men more corrupt than the preceding one. These four historical, or mythical, divisions seem to correspond to a similar division of time, each division, or era, according to Hesiod, lasting one hundred years, and leading with deadly inevitability to the end.

The few fragments of the Tagetic Doctrine that have filtered through to us from Greek and Latin authors indicate to von Vacano that the Etruscan belief in destiny, or fate, was closely linked with the "peculiar method of reckoning time" which they evolved. To begin with, the Etruscans compared the life of a people to the life of a man. Both have a beginning and an end. All that goes between are successive steps on the road to death. The life of the Roman people began with the founding of their city, a date that for the modern world is 753 B.C. For the Romans it was the year One.

The practical Roman mind stressed the beginning, the more imaginative mind of the Etruscan stressed the end. The difference must lie in the fact that for the Roman death *was* the end, while for the Etruscan death meant opening a door into another life that, in the early days, was believed to be as joyous as the life left behind.

Consistent with their belief that "different peoples each had an existence of predetermined duration," the Etruscans held that they had been assigned eight (some traditions say ten) *saecula,* or eras, and, according to Plutarch the year 88 B.C. was the "last year of the eighth *saeculum.*" This was the year when almost all the Etruscans became Roman citizens.

The Etruscans, we learn from surviving fragments of the Tagetic Doctrine, reckoned the passage of time differently from the way the modern world does. For them the length of a *saeculum,* or era, could not be definitely calculated. A *saeculum,* von Vacano explains, "lasted from the end of the preceding one till the death of the last of all those who had been alive at its beginning."

Starting with Plutarch's 88 B.C. and working backward, von Vacano has arrived at a date, 968 B.C., which corresponds for Etruria to Rome's founding date of 753 B.C. von Vacano's method of counting back is interesting. Briefly put, each of the first three ages, the golden, the silver, and the bronze, lasted respectively 119, 119, and 123 years (these figures come from the Latin grammarian Varro); assuming that the age of iron was also 119 years, the figure arrived at is 568 B.C.

Von Vacano then adds Hesiod's four ages, each a hundred years, to 568 and arrives at 968 B.C., the "year in which Etruscan time actually began." This corresponds to the Roman view that regarded the Etruscans as the older race.

"In a world . . . based on subjection to the will of the gods," von Vacano continues, "one thing still remains within the power of the individual man, namely the possibility of getting into communication with the gods. . . . He who does so may, by performing these rites, arrive at such a degree of . . . perfection that some deferment may be granted. . . . though not indeed any absolute reprieve."

Meleager and Adonis each gained a deferment of his fate; Meleager's life was destined to last as long as the log on his mother's hearth-fire remained unburned; Adonis was doomed to six months in the nether world, but with the promise of six months in the light of the sun.

Perugia also gained a deferment; she did not perish in 88 B.C., but in 41 B.C., in the fire set by her loyal citizen Cestio, whose hand the god Tinia may have guided. Perugia's end and that of all Etruria was thought to have been foreshadowed by the great fiery comet that appeared after Caesar's death and that remained visible for seven days. So the "wisest" of the Etruscan seers had prophesied. His people, he stated, had now reached the final stage of earthly life. In this stage the semi-legendary Vegoia predicted men would lie and steal and deceive their fellows, as in the Iron Age that Hesiod so deplored.

To account for the downfall of ancient Etruria, historians have advanced many reasons, yet all acknowledge that the Etruscans were endowed with many of the qualities needed to produce a well-ordered civilization. Highly individualistic and with a sense of purpose that should have carried them as far politically as in those other fields of human achievement in which they excelled, the Etruscans never succeeded in throwing off the shackles, spiritual and material, of the Bronze Age.

To the very end their reason was dominated by a childish subservience to whatever their soothsayers told them had been handed down by their mythical founder, Tages. An example of this subservience, which occurred as late as the fourth century B.C., comes from Livy. Upon one occasion the armies of two Etruscan cities went into battle led by their soothsayers, who wore masks and brandished snakes and lighted torches to frighten the Roman soldiers.

Despite the sense of purpose credited to the Etruscans, they seem never to have understood that only in unity can there be strength. Loose and unorganized, their confederations fell apart under stress. Still, in spite of their disunity and Bronze Age conservatism, the Etruscans might have coalesced into a nation, had it not been for the policy Rome developed slowly over the centuries, a policy the world knows only too well today: divide and conquer. This principle the Etruscans never grasped. So her cities fell, one by one, into the ever-widening maw of insatiable Rome.

The existence of the Etruscans as an ethnic entity lasted only a few hundred years, but the vitalizing current they introduced into the stream of history has never ceased to flow. Uprooted from a land of ancient traditions that lay close to the soil, the Etruscans brought with them to their new home imagination, ideas, and skills that by-passed Roman man, but flowered into life in the mind of medieval man.

The ancient Greek was not by-passed, but unlike the Etruscan, in whose receptive mind the Tagetic Doctrine had inculcated unwavering belief, the Greek had to forge for himself his links with the world about him. In forging his links, the Greek gave us, among other priceless gifts, logic, philosophy, and science, through which they have taught us clarity of thought.

Life for the Etruscan was not thought; it was something that was meant to be lived, and lived to the fullest, through the senses and through the imagination.

In 1848 George Dennis wrote that the excavations in Etruria had yielded so much information that the whole life of Etruscan man, from the "cradle to the grave" lay unrolled before our eyes. Since Dennis's day, the excavations have yielded much more, but we have not yet penetrated the deepest mystery of all, that of the Etruscan heart. For us today then, the mystery still exists, and possibly for the Western mind will always exist, because we have lost that primitive simplicity which could accept the world as a harmonious whole, wherein dualism had no part, since both gods and men were subject to an irrational and incomprehensible fate. Yet in this magico-religious world, where logical thinking was unknown, Etruscan man was taught by the Tagetic Doctrine that he had his assured place, now and hereafter.

Index

Achilles, 99
Acosta, Jorge, 45
Aelian, *History of Animals*, 121
Aeneas, 115, 116
After World, 16, 30, 209–10, 211; banquet scene, 38; concept of, 11; gifts, use of, 39; hut-urns, 41–42; identification, 36, 40; pessimism, 35; subterranean, 21, 36; tomb furniture, 26; traveling to, 24; vision, 28
Agamemnon, 99
Alalia, 142–43
Alba Longa, 115, 138; Castel Gandolfo, 132; destruction of, 132
Alcestis, 97
American Academy in Rome, xvii
Anatolia, xv, 5, 6, 11, 81, 82
Ancients: beliefs, 118, 210–11, in reflections (*anima*), 31; compassion, 111–12; four metal ages, 210–11
Ancus Marcius, King of Rome, 125, 127, 129–30, 176; democratic ideals, 138, 149; rule, 131; sons, 130, 131, 135
Apollo of Veii, discovery, 205
Archaeologists, amateur, 13–14
Archaeology, of Etruria, 7
Ardea, 159, 198; Tarquin attack on, 156, 158
Aristodemus, King of Cumae, 155, 181, 188
Aristotle, 70; music, 100
Arrezzo, 165, 192, 200, 203
Art(s): Etruscan-Greek differences, 98; family life, 66, 67; mythology and, 89–98; nudity, 93; origin, 88; portraiture, 96–97; realism in, 96; wealth of, 87–88
Aruns (son of Tarquin the Proud), 144–47, 155, 173, 174
Ashur-nasir-pal, King, 19
Asphodel, 9
Athrpa mirror, 205, 207–9
Augustus, Emperor, 5, 49, 61, 95, 136, 182, 203; Veii, 192
Aztecs, 45

Babylon, dice, 109
Baker, Kathryn M., xviii
Berlin Museum: hut-urn, 42; Tages mirror, 56
Bloch, Raymond, 165
Blood: Book of the Mummy, 84; significance of, 44–45
Bocchoris tomb (Tarquinia), 19
Bologna (Felsina), founding of, 156
Bonaparte, Lucien, 13, 14
Boni, 40
Book of the Mummy, xvii, 45, 83–84
Bostom Museum of Fine Arts, 19, jewelry, 77
Brennus (the Gaul), 195, 199
Brutus, 173; conspiracy against, 168–69; consul, 166–67, 168, 169; death, 174; revolt against Tarquin, 158 ff. *See* Marcus Lucius Junius
Bulla, 52, 53, 70, 90, 91
Buonarroti family, 41
Burial-urns, 62; variations, 42

Caesar, Julius: assassination, 203; comet, 212
Caligula, Emperor, 143
Calydonian boar-hunt, 205–7
Camillus, Marcus Furius, 191–92; dictator, 198, 199; and Gauls, 198
Campania, 164
Canino, Princess of, 18
Capua, founding of, 164
Carthage, 203; -Rome, 202; sea power, 75
Castellani collection, 77
Certosa *situla*, 121–22
Cerveteri (Caere), 7, 13, 14, 80, 159, 165, 168; Campana Tomb, 27; grave-mounds, 8–9; location, 16; prosperity, 75; revolt against Rome, 140; sarcophagus (Louvre), 33; Tarquin the Proud, 163, 176; Tomb of the Little House (or Cottage), 26; Tomb of the Reliefs, 26; Tomb of the Sarcophagi, 29; Tomb of the Tarquins, 29; tombs, 23; Vestal Virgins, 196

215